B-2A SPIRIT
UNITS IN COMBAT

GH00568987

SERIES EDITOR: TONY HOLMES

OSPREY COMBAT AIRCRAFT • 64

B-2A SPIRIT
UNITS IN COMBAT

Thomas Withington

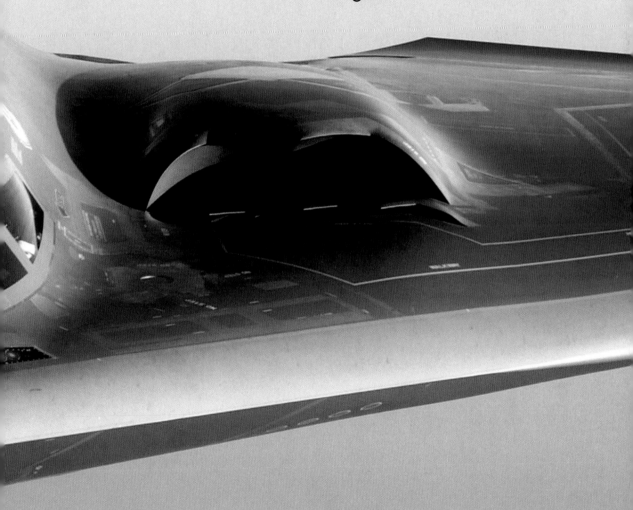

OSPREY
PUBLISHING

First published in Great Britain in 2006 by Osprey Publishing
Midland House, West Way, Botley, Oxford, OX2 0PH
443 Park Avenue South, New York, NY, 10016, USA

ISBN 10: 1-84176-993-2
ISBN 13: 978-1-84176-993-6

Edited by Tony Holmes
Page design by Mark Holt
Typeset in Adobe Garamond, Rockwell and Univers
Aircraft Profiles by Chris Davey
Scale Drawings by Mark Styling
Index by Alan Thatcher
Originated by United Graphics, Singapore
Printed in China through Bookbuilders

06 07 08 09 10   10 9 8 7 6 5 4 3 2 1

For a catalogue of all books published by Osprey please contact:
NORTH AMERICA
Osprey Direct, C/o Random House Distribution Center,
400 Hahn Road, Westminster, MD 21157
E-mail:info@ospreydirect.com

ALL OTHER REGIONS
Osprey Direct UK, P.O. Box 140 Wellingborough, Northants, NN8 2FA, UK
E-mail: info@ospreydirect.co.uk
www.ospreypublishing.com

EDITOR'S NOTE
To make this best-selling series as authoritative as possible, the Editor would
be interested in hearing from anyone who may have relevant photographs,
documentation or first-hand experiences relating to pilots, and their aircraft,
of the various theatres of war. Please write to Tony Holmes via e-mail
at:tony.holmes@osprey-jets.freeserve.co.uk

ACKNOWLEDGEMENTS
I am indebted to the following individuals for their generous assistance in the
production of this book – Maj Joe P Dellavedova and his colleagues at the Public
Affairs Office for the 509th Bomb Wing (BW) at Whiteman Air Force Base (AFB);
Col Eric Single, Vice Commander of the 509th BW; Lt Cols Steve Basham and
Thomas Bussiere, Commanders of the 393rd and 13th BSs respectively; Capt Adam
'Shift' Cuquet, 394th Combat Training Squadron (CTS); Capt Patrick McMahon,
37th Bomb Squadron (BS); Chief Master Sergeants Beau Turner and Kelly Costa
of the 509th Maintenance Group; James 'Jim' Kinnu and Irving 'Irv' Waaland;
Michael Rich of the RAND Corporation; James F Hart of the Northrop Grumman
Corporation; Ted Carlson and last but by no means least Nathalie Riveré de Carles
for her unending motivation and support. Every effort has been made to ensure
the utmost accuracy of this work and any mistakes are solely the responsibility
of the author.

CONTENTS

DEVELOPMENT HISTORY

'B-2 or not B-2, that is the question. Whether 'tis nobler in the mind to suffer the slings and arrows of outrageous expense, or to take arms against a sea of deficits, and by opposing end them. To cut, to spend no more, and by a cut to say we end the heartache and a thousand cost overruns that B-2 is heir to.'

The words of Congressman Edward J Markey to the House of Representatives during a critical debate on the B-2A Spirit stealth bomber may have had more of a trace of irony. Echoing the famous words of The Bard, the Northrop B-2A Spirit, like Hamlet, also looked (budgetary) death in the face on numerous occasions, but unlike the Dane survived the political slings and arrows. The Advanced Technology Bomber project – which would become the B-2 programme – would go from experiencing Shakespearean plot to Kafkaesque secrecy.

INVISIBILITY

Avoiding radar is an ambition almost as old as the hills in the world of military aviation. The discovery of radar by the British on the eve of World War 2 would provide a breakthrough for the detection of aircraft in the short term, and would change the face of air power in the long term. Prior to its invention, air power thinkers such as Gen Guilio Douhet argued that there was no defence against massed raids of bombers given that they would only be detected once they attacked, and that they would have escaped back to the safety of home before fighter aircraft could intercept them.

The popular phrase of the time, coined by the British Prime Minister Stanley Baldwin, was that the 'bomber will always get through' – something that has become a reality with the B-2A. If any event ever illustrated the value of radar, it was the Battle of Britain in the summer of 1940, during which the Royal Air Force was able to get advanced warning of the arrival of Luftwaffe aircraft thanks to radar. Such a capability was decisive.

As early as 1935, Sir Robert Watson-Watt, the leading pioneer of radar, had already observed that it would be imperative in the future for bombers to be designed in such a fashion as to reduce their radar reflectivity – more commonly known as their 'radar signature'. Yet Sir Robert's theories remained just that. Aircraft designers had not yet mastered how to measure their aircraft's radar reflections. Furthermore, after 1939 there was a war to be won, and radar reflectivity took a back seat in comparison to designing fast and robust fighters which could shoot down the enemy.

That is not to say that anti-radar reflectivity efforts remained static. The skill of German aviation engineers during World War 2 is now legendary and thoroughly documented, and one important effort to cut radar signature was made by German brothers Walter and Reimer Horten. Eight years after Sir Robert Watson-Watt's announcements on the importance of signature reduction, they produced a twin-engined flying wing reconnaissance aircraft and bomber which was known as the Ho 1X, and was later redesignated as the Gotha Go 229.

The Hortens had already realised how vital the correct materials would be in reducing signatures. They constructed their aircraft from plywood which was cemented with glue, sawdust and charcoal which could absorb radar waves. But given that Nazi Germany was suffering from a shortage of war materials, and was also feeling the squeeze of the Allied grip, the top brass desisted from building a large fleet of such aircraft.

On the other side of the Atlantic a certain Jack Northrop was also turning his thoughts towards flying wing aircraft. The legendary designer had been thinking about flying wings since the 1920s, and by the time World War 2 had broken out he was able to begin building one. Always on the look out for new ideas, the US Government commissioned him to build the piston-engined XB-35 experimental bomber. However, towards the end of the war jet engine technology was maturing, and the government gave Jack Northrop a contract to build 13 YB/YBR-49 jet-powered flying wing bombers. The government later reneged on the deal, cancelled the order and the airframes were destroyed.

Jack Northrop's ideas were way ahead of their time. A series of prototype airframes were designed but with none getting to the production stage. Their amazing shape, however, was not lost on Hollywood, and the YB-49 design features in the 1959 epic *War of the Worlds* in which its nuclear attack fails to stop the Martians.

One of the first US attempts to reduce radar signatures came with Project *Harvey* which began in 1974. Named after a James Stewart film about a giant invisible rabbit, this initiative was to study ideas for building an aircraft that could ensure its survival by using stealth technology alone. To this end, the Defence Advanced Research Projects Agency (DARPA) awarded a contract to Northrop and McDonnell Douglas. The aviation rumour network ensured that Lockheed got wind of *Harvey* and subsequently paid out of their own funds to participate in the initiative. Fortune smiled on Northrop and Lockheed and both companies were commissioned by DARPA to build a stealthy demonstration aircraft known as the 'Experimental Survivable Testbed' (XST). McDonnell Douglas, meanwhile, found itself out of the stealth aircraft business.

XST did not produce working aircraft, the two companies instead building mock-ups which could be tested for resistance to radar waves at the Radar Target Scatter – known as the 'RATSCAT' – at Holloman AFB, New Mexico.

Other American stealth initiatives included the reconfiguration of BQM-34 'Firebee' target drones,

Bearing an uncanny resemblance to the shape which would emerge four decades later as the B-2A, Northrop's XB-35 was a vital leap forward in terms of understanding flying wing technology. The design was so ground breaking, however, that the Air Force's top brass was frequently undecided as to whether it would take the design forward into production. It would take Northrop until the 1970s to convince them (*Northrop Grumman*)

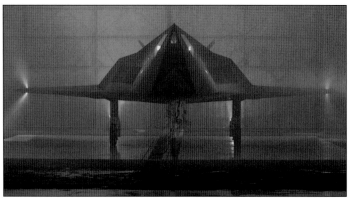

Representing two very different approaches to the stealth phenomena, the F-117A Nighthawk's angular appearance distorts radar waves and scatters their returns. The B-2A and the Nighthawk would represent two very different, but equally complimentary, approaches for out-smarting radar (*Lockheed Martin*)

which had been modified for reconnaissance missions with the installation of layers of Radar Absorbing Materials (RAMs) to cover their fuselages. Wire mesh was also fitted over the engine intakes in an effort to hide engine compressor blades from the gaze of radar. The Lockheed SR-71A reconnaissance aircraft also had stealthy characteristics, but primarily relied on high-speed and high-altitude flight to avoid being downed by Soviet air defences.

Part of the reason as to why Low-Observable (LO) technology took so long to perfect was because the mystical properties of radar were still being unravelled. In 1966, computer scientist Denys Overholser translated the seminal paper of physicist Pyotr Ufimtsev on radar technology. Overholser's interpretation led to him devising a computer programme known as ECHO 1, which is said to have provided the answer as to how an aircraft's shape could be improved to make it more resilient to radar detection.

The work of Overholser would become the basis for the *Have Blue* programme, which would later become the Lockheed F-117A Nighthawk stealth fighter. The company had been selected to build a flying XST in March 1976, and subsequently built two *Have Blue* prototypes. Northrop had also participated in the programme, but lost out to its Lockheed counterparts.

Irving 'Irv' Waaland, the Chief Designer of the B-2A for Northrop, remembers how his company became involved with stealth;

'The first thing we worked on was a competition for what ended up as the F-117 fighter, and Northrop was the loser against Lockheed. All we did during that project was to build a full scale model of the proposed design and test it for radar cross section, as well as wind tunnel testing and so forth. There was no aeroplane built for the competition, but when Lockheed won, it built the *Have Blue* demonstrator. But we had done well enough in the competition, and the technology was a great interest to the government. The conclusion was anything in the future which was of a combat nature should incorporate stealth technology, and the government did not want to have a single contractor responsible.'

DARPA asked Northrop to stick around, and in December 1976 instructed it to undertake a study to build a stealthy design for a so-called 'Assault Breaker' initiative. This effort was not to be a stand-alone aircraft, but was instead envisaged as a 'suite' of initiatives which would use 'smart' weapons mounted on a deep-penetrating strike platform. Moreover, Assault Breaker would use state-of-the-art sensors and electronics to disrupt the ISTAR (Intelligence, Surveillance, Target Acquisition and Reconnaissance) efforts of the Soviets forces during any confrontation on the central European plain.

Waaland recalls that DARPA 'had invited us in to discuss another application because it had a Low Probability of Intercept radar and it wanted to integrate that radar with an aircraft. It wanted a design that would operate parallel to enemy airspace rather than penetrating it. So, instead of a low-radar cross section to the front and rear, DARPA also wanted it to the side too. We started activity on the jet in mid 1977, and we were quite successful in coming up with a design that was called Battlefield Surveillance Aircraft Experimental (BSAX). We put in a proposal towards the end of 1977, and in January 1978 I was advised that Northrop had been given the contract. Four months later we were given a contract for what was called *Tacit Blue*.'

Northrop's design was one of the most bizarre looking aircraft ever to grace the skies, with 'whale' and 'flying bathtub' being just some of the monikers that the *Tacit Blue* jet received – one comment even described it as being the 'ugliest aircraft ever built'. This prototype performed 134 flights before the programme was cancelled. It was replaced by a battlefield surveillance programme which would be mounted on a Boeing 707 airframe and which would later become known as the E-8C Joint Surveillance Target Attack Radar System. *Tacit Blue* would not see the light of day until 1996 when it was unveiled to the public and put on display at the USAF Museum at Wright Patterson AFB, Ohio.

Tacit Blue would pave the way for the B-2A Spirit. 'In April 1979, we were so successful with *Tacit Blue* that DARPA wanted us to do a bomber, and our initial response was that we were not really a bomber house, we were more a fighter house, but by June they had convinced the company that they really should get into it', recalled Irv Waaland.

One year before the *Tacit Blue* programme began at Northrop, the Pentagon, and in particular the then Secretary of Defense William 'Bill' Perry in the administration of President Jimmy Carter, had become very interested in stealth technology. Perry and his colleagues were especially concerned that advancements in Soviet air defences might eventually render the US bomber force impotent. Stealth technology applied to jets would obviate this advantage, enabling a stealth aircraft to penetrate the Warsaw Pact air defence radar screen without needing a huge strike package of electronic warfare and defence suppression aircraft to ensure its safety.

The birth of the B-2A is also owed to an event in 1977 – 30 June to be precise – when President Carter cancelled the Rockwell B-1A Advanced Manned Strategic Aircraft and directed that no further B-1As be built. The sop given to the USAF was that they would continue to be allowed to test the aircraft, and later, under the administration of President Ronald Reagan, would resurrect it as the improved Rockwell B-1B Lancer bomber.

At the time, it was said that Carter had little faith in heavy bombers for the nuclear attack mission, believing instead that Air-Launched Cruise Missiles (ALCMs) would be able to perform the job better with no risk to aircrew. That said, Carter did not dismiss bombers out of hand. He ordered funds to be redirected from the B-1A programme to modify B-52G/H Stratofortress bombers to carry ALCMs. These aircraft would operate with nuclear-armed General Dynamics FB-111A aircraft as well as Submarine-Launched Ballistic Missiles (SLBMs) and land-based Intercontinental Ballistic Missiles (ICBMs). Yet there was a problem with the air component of this strategy. Even back then, the B-52 was not exactly a young aircraft, while the FB-111A was at best only ever a medium bomber lacking the range and payload of its heavier sibling.

For its part, the USAF ordered a number of studies to find a replacement for the B-52. These studies culminated in an alphabet soup of acronyms –

Although Northrop's BSAX *Tacit Blue* was not the prettiest aircraft ever devised, it gave the manufacturer a much better understanding of stealth technology. Several stealthy 'giveaways' can be seen in the design from the split tail, reminiscent of the F-117A, to the cockpit design. *Tacit Blue* also had a recessed engine inlet in the upper fuselage – the B-2A has a similar design for its engines, which are also recessed into the wings (*USAF*)

the MRB (Multi-Role Bomber), SWL (Strategic Weapons Launcher), NPT (Near-Term Penetrator), LRCA (Long-Range Combat Aircraft) and the CMCA (Cruise Missile Carrier Aircraft). These studies yielded a cornucopia of aircraft design concepts from high-and-fast, and low-and-slow nuclear-armed penetrating aircraft, flying-wing designs and even some bereft of wings altogether. As cruise missile carriers, the USAF contemplated arming an airliner – either Boeing 747, Lockheed L-1011 or a McDonnell Douglas DC-10 airframe

USAF stealth side by side. Both the F-117A and B-2A airframes complement each other, despite their radically different sizes and shapes. Between the two aircraft, they can perform stealthy ground attack missions across the entire tactical and strategic spectrums (*SSgt Bernard Wilson*)

– with cruise missiles. Yet these aircraft would not exactly be inconspicuous on Soviet radar screens, even when flying at stand-off ranges, and this idea was scrapped.

Carter had a secret weapon. Despite sustaining heavy criticism for his decision to stop the B-1A programme, and receiving accusations from the Republican Party that he was 'soft on defence', he was in possession of powerful information which he could not discuss.

Some of the money that Carter had saved from cancelling the B-1A was channelled into a new project called the Advanced Strategic Penetrator Aircraft (ASPA), which would produce studies on a low-observable, long-range strike aircraft that was initially earmarked for a production run of 132 examples. His defence policy was one of the things that got Carter voted out of office, to be followed by the more hawkish Ronald Reagan and the commencement of the 'Second Cold War'. Reagan had little hesitation in authorising the commencement of the Advanced Technology Bomber (ATB) programme which turned the ASPA studies into a firm aircraft project.

Lockheed and Northrop were invited to tender for the ATB programme, and each company proposed a radically different design. The former went with a scaled-up version of its F-117A, given the codename *Senior Peg*. For Northrop, the company went back to its work on flying wings.

'We looked at two concepts, one of which was a penetrating, low altitude aircraft like the B-1 that would take advantage of low-level flying as well as stealth. The other was flying high enough with a low radar cross-section to avoid detection. The latter was a similar shape to what the B-2 is today, with an inboard diamond and an outboard swept wing. We briefed that idea to the Department of Defense (DoD), and they were interested and said to pursue the high-altitude approach, and we went back and submitted the proposals for concept development', recalled Irv Waaland.

This was arguably a much more radical option. The costs involved in developing flying wings had, at times, come close to ruining the company financially. Moreover, the USAF had frequently run hot and cold in its feelings for such unorthodox designs since the late 1940s. The YB-49 would provide the template for the Northrop concept, and it has been said that the original flying wing had shown itself to be very hard to detect when viewed by radar from different angles.

In terms of capabilities, the USAF wanted an aircraft that could perform nuclear strike, conventional attack, anti-shipping missions, maritime patrol and sea-mining. It had to be capable of performing these mission unsupported against air defences, and also have the ability to autonomously detect both fixed- and mobile targets. The assumed greater importance when, in the late 1970s and early 1980s, it became apparent that the USSR was doing its best to make its nuclear weapons as hard to find as possible by making them mobile. For instance, the SS-25 ICBM is mounted on a wheeled Transporter-Erector-Launcher, while the SS-24 was housed in a special train. Looking for a moving target in the Soviet Union would be like looking for a drifting needle in a haystack.

There was also some 'requirement creep' in developing the aircraft. Originally, the bomber was to have a 'high-high-high' mission profile – high-altitude flight to the target, high-altitude weapons release and high-altitude egress. The USAF top brass then decided that the aircraft should also have a residual low-altitude target penetration capability just in case the Soviets wised up and developed the technology to accurately detect the jet.

'This imposed certain requirements on the structure and on the control systems. The control system was what we called an Active Control System in that it not only flew the aeroplane, it also provided the capability to alleviate load when you hit a sharp edge gust', explained Northrop Grumman's B-2A Project Manager, James 'Jim' Kinnu.

'The capability of the aeroplane was always to have the ability to perform a mission in a conventional war. That's why we fitted both a rotary launcher and a bomb rack', Kinnu concluded. Conventional capabilities were imperative for the aircraft. Not only should the ATB be capable of unleashing atomic weapons, but also to destroy key enemy installations with conventional bombs before a nuclear exchange.

Such was the complexity of developing the aircraft that Northrop and Lockheed 'teamed up' with other aerospace firms (Boeing and Rockwell respectively) while they were drafting their bids in order to spread the task of designing and producing such a huge undertaking. This also helped to spread some of the risk. Such was the investment that a project like this required that its termination at any point could prove fatal to a supplier if it was fulfilling the contract alone. 'We knew that the job was more than we could handle ourselves so we added some partners. We added the Boeing company as the primary subcontractor', remembered Irv Waaland. Engine builders Pratt & Whitney and General Electric competed to see who would supply the engines.

Building on its flying wing expertise, Northrop proposed a flying wing design with buried engines – six to be precise. The idea was for the aircraft to be very thin when viewed from the front and side, yet it would not retain such wafer-thin characteristics. After all, it had to carry weapons which would necessitate a relatively deep fuselage.

Taxiing for take-off, the first ever B-2 prepares for its maiden flight from the Air Force Flight Test Centre at Edwards AFB, California, on 17 July 1989 (*Alan Wycheck*)

Irv Waaland recalled that the Pentagon 'had certain requirements that they laid out. They wanted 6000 miles of range, non-stop, unrefuelled, with 10,000 lbs of payload. We decided that two crew members would probably be adequate for the aeroplane. But Strategic Air Command (SAC) felt that the payload was far too small, and instead of a single bomb bay we changed to two bomb-bays which could carry 20,000 lbs of ordnance between them. The wind tunnel tests were good. We selected an engine which was a derivative of the General Electric F110 powerplant, which has much the same core as the engine used by the B-1B. It was a good engine for high-altitude operations'.

Full contract award was 'on 1 December 1980. The day that we had gotten the call that we had been awarded the contract was quite an exuberant one because Northrop had not won a major contract for quite a few years for a first-line weapons system development programme. It had been a major corporate objective for years to obtain just such a contract. It was a major win for all of us. There was great enthusiasm, but it had to stay inside the building, given the secrecy of the programme'.

Lockheed would be out of the military jet building business until it subsequently won contracts for the F-22A Raptor and the F-35A Joint Strike Fighter.

Northrop placed its aircraft under a top-secret designation known as 'Senior CJ', the latter initials being taken from Connie Jo Kelly, a secretary in the Pentagon stealth programme office. Jack Northrop, the company's founder and father of the flying wing, was informed of the ATB bid shortly before he died in February 1981, saying that 'now I know why God has kept me alive for the past 25 years'.

From this point, the contract went into the black, and also into the red, as a cloak of secrecy was placed around the ATB initiative and costs began to mount. The B-2A was not always as 'black' as one might have thought. Rumours circulated throughout the 1980s of the aircraft's existence, while artists' impressions and model kits would often bear an uncanny resemblance to the finished product. That said, Northrop took extraordinary measures to ensure that the project remained top secret.

A separate division of the company called 'Advanced Projects' was established to manage the programme, and it would be housed at a former Ford Motor Company factory at Pico Rivera, California. The site was surrounded by razor wire and high-tech security systems, James Kinnu recalling that 'we bought it, tore it apart and then rebuilt it. We also had to construct a facility at Palmdale for the US government in which to build the aircraft'.

Irv Waaland remembered that the secrecy surrounding the programme could be time consuming;

'We had to do background checks on personnel, and it took time to take people on. Every piece of paper that was generated had to go through security, so you couldn't just hand anything to anyone else. However, we had secure computer connections set up between us, the primary subcontractors and the government. Every night, all the information on the programme was updated at all the locations.'

Behind the security systems was hard work and high technology. The Boeing 777 airliner is often said to have been the first aircraft to be designed entirely by computer. This is not strictly true. Northrop developed a series of advanced computer modelling design tools to get the stealth bomber flying. 'We were doing all of this on computers, and nobody had ever done it this way before', explained James Kinnu. 'We used a system called NCAD, which was developed by Northrop Grumman, and we shared that with Boeing and Vought (another B-2A subcontractor) because they didn't have such equipment – in fact, nobody in the industry did. We were developing the drawing system at the same time we were developing the aircraft! We had enough of a capability at the beginning, and then we just added to NCAD as designers sought ways to improve it'.

Each component used in the aircraft's construction had its characteristics logged on a database as part of the company's Computer-Integrated Manufacturing system. This enabled engineers to see on a computer screen how a set of components would actually fit together before assembly would take place. Materials science also took a quantum leap forward with carbon fibre being used throughout the aircraft, which helped to absorb radar signals and was easier to machine than metal.

Early on in the project Northrop Grumman electrical engineer Fred Oshira invented the so-called 'Source Distribution Technique', which could demonstrate the radar cross-sections of surfaces through the use of a computer. Moreover, this electronic information could be encrypted and transmitted to other engineers working on the ATB at the subcontractor level. Although much of the development work associated with the B-2 remains classified, what is known is that the programme was responsible for a major advancement not only in materials science and manufacturing techniques, but also in aerodynamics and defence aerospace electronics.

Seven years after Northrop was awarded the ATB project, the world was able to see the fruits of its labour on 22 November 1988 at the company's Plant 42 at Palmdale, California. Air Vehicle One (AV-1/82-1066 *SPIRIT OF AMERICA*) was towed out of the hangar and unveiled to the world. Never had such an aircraft been seen in the flesh before, and never had a more futuristic design been devised. Rivalling Concorde for its timeless beauty, the dark, sinister shape basked in the bright west coast sunshine. But the secrecy remained. Spectators were kept 200 ft from the jet, and the design was only shown from the front.

This did not stop enterprising *Aviation Week & Space Technology* journalist Michael A Dornheim from hiring a light aircraft to over-fly the plant and photograph the now-christened B-2A Spirit from above, aft end and all, fully visible. There was nothing illegal about Dornheim's actions, no doubt much to the frustration of the USAF and Northrop, but his publication soon gained the nickname 'Aviation Leak'.

While Northrop had been building its aircraft, the Pentagon had been busying itself with the question of where such a bomber would be based. Congressman Ike Skelton duly announced that Whiteman AFB, Missouri, would be the home of the B-2A on 5 January 1987. The bomber would be placed under the responsibility of the 509th BW, which had been known in the past as the 509th Bombardment Wing (Heavy) and the 509th Composite Wing, the latter being responsible for dropping the atomic bombs on Hiroshima and Nagasaki which ended World War 2.

In the flat Mid-West, Missouri was an appropriate home for the aircraft. The B-2A would be the first bomber that the 509th had

Air power will never be the same again – the B-2A is rolled-out in front of the world for the first time at Northrop's Plant 42 in Palmdale amid tight security and a sense of astonishment on 22 November 1988 (*MSgt Patrick Nugent*)

Whiteman AFB, Missouri, was chosen as the aircraft's home some 19 months prior to the B-2 making its first flight. The wide wingspan of the bomber can be clearly seen in proportion to the width of the taxiway at its home hase. 82-1070 *SPIRIT OF OHIO* was briefly given the nickname *FIRE & ICE* (and associated artwork, seen here on its nosewheel door) during climatic tests as part of Exercise *Frozen Spirit 96*, staged at Eielson AFB, Alaska (*USAF*)

possessed since the 1960s, when it flew B-47 Stratojets prior to trading these in for Minuteman ICBMs. The base was an ideal choice, being located almost smack-bang in the middle of the United States, and far enough away to avoid an attack from SLBMs. It was also slightly further east, and hence slightly closer to targets in the USSR, than the other candidate bases in Oklahoma and Texas. Moreover, Whiteman had more than enough room for growth and improvement.

The first unit to be stood up with B-2As was the 393rd BS 'Tigers', closely followed by the 394th Combat Training Squadron (CTS) and the 325th BS 'Alley Oop'. The latter unit was redesignated as the 13th BS in September 2005. Each squadron is responsible for eight B-2A aircraft.

As the 509th was preparing to receive its new aircraft, testing of AV-1 continued unabated. The jet first performed taxi trials on 10 July 1989, during which it reached a maximum speed of 103 mph. Six days later, the aircraft was given permission to make its first test flight, with Northrop Chief Test Pilot for the B-2A, Bruce J Hinds, and USAF Director of the B-2 Combined Test Force, Col Richard S Couch, at the controls.

By November 1989 the aircraft had flown six missions. Yet while the jet was still being tested, the political wrangling over the aircraft's massive cost continued, and would culminate in Secretary of Defense Richard B Cheney making an announcement that the original order for 132 aircraft would be downgraded to 76. This was the first of two cuts in the number of aircraft that would be procured. In January 1991, the USAF announced that it expected the cost of developing the infrastructure for 76 B-2As would be $648 billion in 1991 dollars.

The B-2A did not escape the axe for long, and in January 1992 the orders for the aircraft hit rock-bottom with a firm commitment to just 20 aircraft, plus a single test example which would not be upgraded to an

operational level. The reduced order brought the support price tag for the aircraft down to a more modest, yet still massive, $45.3 billion in 1992 dollars. In the intervening period, the Soviet Union had collapsed, leading to an increased emphasis being placed on the conventional abilities of the aircraft.

Nuclear war, always a major part of the aircraft's *raison d'etre*, was now a distant possibility. However, the debate did not end. In 1994, Chairman of the House Senate National Security Committee, Floyd D Spence, went on record to disagree with capping the programme at 20 jets, stating that it was a 'political decision, and does not make a lot of sense from a strategic or operational perspective'.

DELIVERIES

The first operational B-2A delivered to the 509thBW was AV-8/88-0329 *SPIRIT OF MISSOURI*, which arrived at Whiteman on 17 December 1993. This was followed by AV-9/88-0330 *SPIRIT OF CALIFORNIA* on 17 August 1994, AV-7/88-0328 *SPIRIT OF TEXAS* 16 days later, AV-11/88-0332 *SPIRIT OF WASHINGTON* in late October and AV-10/88-0331 *SPIRIT OF SOUTH CAROLINA* by the end of the year.

The aircraft was now in the hands of the USAF, and it soon put the B-2 through its paces to see what it was capable of. On 12 January 1995, the 509th BW launched a trio of aircraft in just over 30 minutes. The three Spirits duly completed air-to-air refuelling operations, practised bomb runs and set a record for six B-2A sorties in one day. Eleven days later, the aircraft made an appearance at the legendary *Red Flag* exercise at Nellis AFB, Nevada, during which an undisclosed number of bombers participated in a NATO-style combined air warfare exercise until 15 February.

On 11 June 1995, 88-0329 *SPIRIT OF MISSOURI* made the B-2's first appearance outside the USA when it made a 1-hour and 20-minute visit to the 41st Paris Salon. The jet had flown one of its longest missions to date to participate in the event, thus demonstrating to the world its 'Global Power' capabilities (*SRA Diane S Robinson*)

88-0332 *SPIRIT OF WASHINGTON* departs from the Nellis runway during a *Red Flag* exercise. The B-2A participated in these legendary exercises at an early stage in its career, no doubt in order to fully familiarise other NATO and Allied air forces, and the USAF, with the peculiarities of operating with the Spirit (*USAF*)

Forty-eight hours later, the wing received AV-12/89-0127 *SPIRIT OF KANSAS* and AV-13/89-0128 *SPIRIT OF NEBRASKA*, followed by AV-14/89-0129 *SPIRIT OF GEORGIA* on 14 November 1995.

The B-2A's travel scheduled was non-stop, and on 11 June 1995 the aircraft flew directly to the Paris Airshow from Whiteman. If ever anyone needed proof of the bomber's global reach, then this was it. With Brig Gen Ronald Marcotte and Maj Jim Smithers in the cockpit, the B-2 overflew the event and then landed in Paris for a one-hour stop, during which the engines remained active, the crew was changed and the jet flew all the way back to Whiteman – all-in-all the mission added up to a 25-hour exercise. A feat of airmanship, but a comparatively short work-out compared to some of the flights which the B-2A would make once in combat.

A similarly exhausting mission was performed by 89-0127 *SPIRIT OF KANSAS* when, in September, it flew to Honolulu in Hawaii to celebrate the Allies' triumph over Japan in World War 2. This was also the first time that the B-2A had performed a mission over the Pacific Ocean.

Ironically, the first B-2A received in 1996 was AV-16/90-0041 *SPIRIT OF HAWAII*, which arrived at Whiteman on 10 January, closely followed by AV-15/90-0040 *SPIRIT OF ALASKA* 14 days later.

Early that year, a two-aircraft formation of B-2As flew to Andersen AFB, Guam, in the Pacific Ocean – a base which would become a regular home for the aircraft in subsequent exercises. A single aircraft continued on to the Asian Aerospace air show in Singapore, while the other singleton conducted practice missions from Andersen AFB.

A similar mission was performed when 88-0332 *SPIRIT OF WASHINGTON* flew to the FIDAE '96 event in Santiago, Chile, in March 1996, setting the record for the longest B-2A mission to date. 1996 also saw the delivery of the 11th aircraft, AV-18/93-1085 *SPIRIT OF OKLAHOMA* on 15 May, with AV-17/92-0700 arriving on 3 July. The final delivery for the 509th in 1996 was of AV-19/93-1086 *SPIRIT OF KITTY HAWK*.

During that same year, the wing began to receive some of the all important weaponry which would give the B-2A its conventional punch. Between 8 and 12 July, the 509th took delivery of GBU-36/37 Global Positioning System (GPS) aided bombs. On 17 September, the wing performed a drop of inert versions of the weapon when three bombers delivered ordnance reaching a proximity of four feet from a ground target on the test range at Nellis AFB. This was a remarkable feat, and beared witness to the highly sophisticated guidance systems on the aircraft and on the weapons.

One of the aircraft involved in the mission dropped 16 GBU-37s against 16 different targets from an altitude of 40,000 ft which resulted in 16 targets destroyed. This sortie secured yet another record for the B-2A, as this was the largest number of precision weapons released at the same time from a single aircraft. Chief of Air Combat Command, Gen Richard Hawley, was moved to declare a limited operational capability for the B-2 and the wing based on the results of these test drops.

Shortly after its forays on the range at Nellis, the B-2A recorded its 1000th sortie with Col James R Macon and Maj Len Litton in the cockpit of the *SPIRIT OF WASHINGTON*. The deliveries for the 509th in 1997 included ex-development aircraft AV-5/82-1070 *SPIRIT OF OHIO*, which arrived

Gen Richard E Hawley, Commander Air Combat Command, shakes hands with North Carolina's Governor Jim Hunt during the dedication ceremonies for B-2A 93-1086 *SPIRIT OF KITTY HAWK*, parked in the background (*SRA Frank P Rizzo*)

Another bomber arrives – from left to right, US Representative John Boehner, Senator Mike De Wine, Senator John Glenn, Secretary of the Air Force Sheila Widnall, Lt Gen Brett Dula (Vice Commander Air Combat Command) Lt Gen Kenneth Eickmann (Commander, Aeronautical Systems Centre) and Kent Keresa (Chairman, President and Chief Executive Officer Northrop Corporation) stand in front of the main undercarriage door during the naming of the *SPIRIT OF OHIO* (*Chris Liptock*)

on 18 July, AV-20/93-1087 *SPIRIT OF PENNSYLVANIA*, delivered on 5 August, ex-development aircraft AV-3/82-1068 *SPIRIT OF NEW YORK*, delivered on 10 October and AV-21/93-1088 *SPIRIT OF LOUISIANA*, delivered one month later. The final B-2A delivery for 1997 was ex-development aircraft AV-4/82-1069 *SPIRIT OF INDIANA* which arrived on 4 December.

The long flights of the B-2A were not just conducted in the air, as the simulator at Whiteman was also getting a good workout. Indeed, Maj Steve Moulton and Capt Jeff Long performed a 44.4-hour simulator mission, which at that time set the record for the longest flight of its type ever. 1997 would also see the 509th BW declare an Initial Operational Capability on 1 April.

The record-breaking bomber was unstoppable. The epic flight to Chile was bettered by Maj Scott Kramer and Capt Jeff Long in May 1997 when they flew a 29.9 hour sortie from Whiteman to RAF Mildenhall's air fete in Suffolk. During the mission, the crew also practised bomb runs over the Continental United States (CONUS). And the duo who had performed the legendary simulator flight returned to the flightdeck to perform a 37.5-hour mission from Whiteman to a bombing range on Guam, where they released a GBU-37, before returning home.

The B-2A was in the peculiar position of being an aircraft which was undergoing testing, while also being inducted into service. In July 1997, the flight testing programme for the bomber was declared to have been a success, with the jet having met all of its design and operational parameters. A total of six aircraft had been used during the testing programme at Edwards AFB, California, these being the *SPIRIT OF MISSOURI*, *SPIRIT OF CALIFORNIA*, *SPIRIT OF TEXAS*, *SPIRIT OF WASHINGTON*, *SPIRIT OF SOUTH CAROLINA* and *SPIRIT OF KANSAS*.

The final deliveries for the 509th included ex-development aircraft, AV-2/82-1067 *SPIRIT OF ARIZONA*, delivered on 4 December 1997, AV-6/82-1071 *SPIRIT OF MISSISSIPPI*, delivered on 23 May 1998 and AV-1/82-1066 *SPIRIT OF AMERICA*, delivered in early 2000. Ironically, the latter jet was the first B-2A to be built but the last to be delivered.

THE DESIGN

Needless to say, the Spirit is one of the most uniquely designed aircraft ever. The targeting pods and external ordnance which are commonplace on today's combat aircraft are absent from the Spirit, and not without good reason, as such additions significantly magnify the aircraft's radar signature, negating the advantages of its design.

The aircraft's flying wing shape was specifically chosen to minimise its appearance from long distances, which also reduced the aircraft's radar cross-section. Moreover, the shape of the aircraft, when viewed from above, presents angles that causes radar signals to be reflected in such a way as to cancel out the signature. The B-2A is remarkable as being an aircraft which looks vastly different from whichever angle it is viewed from. The only part of the aircraft rising from the flat design is the fuselage, which is smoothly blended into the wing.

This intriguing shape presents some challenges to the aircrew given that it makes the aircraft inherently unstable. Because of the shape, the aircraft is unstable in flight. This means that it has to be controlled by a complex fly-by-wire (FBW) system in order to keep the jet from spiralling out of control and plunging to the ground. This system transmits commands to the eight flaps on the aircraft's trailing edges to provide lift or drag on take-off and landing, while also controlling the rudderons which deal with yaw. Flaps located behind the aircraft's engine exhausts can be moved up or down to direct the exhaust which is sticking to the trailing edge of the wing thanks to the Coanda effect. This gives the B-2 thrust-vectoring capability.

The rudderon is a relatively simple device which moves up or down. When used as an airbrake, the rudderons both move up causing the aircraft to slow down. When turning, one rudderon will open causing the opposing side of the aircraft to dip, thus allowing it to turn. However, employment of the rudderon comes with a catch, as using them minimises the stealthiness of the aircraft. There is a way around this, once

The B-2A's shape was purposely designed to minimise the aircraft's appearance in the visual, audio and electronic spectrums. At a distance, the Spirit is almost wafer-thin in silhouette. This is in contrast to when the aircraft is viewed from above, when it seems to retain near 'Manta Ray' characteristics (*USAF*)

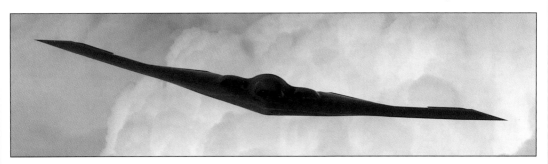

This view of 82-1071 *SPIRIT OF MISSISSIPPI* of the 325th/13th BS gives a good impression of just how smoothly the aircraft's fuselage has been blended into the overall airframe. At first glance, the cockpit area barely seems to elevate above the wing. The shape has been humorously referred to as 'like a slug sitting on a boomerang' (*USAF*)

in combat, as the engines can be used to control the yaw of the aircraft – more power on the right engine will cause the aircraft to move left, and vice versa.

In terms of structural designs, the B-2 uses carbon fibre and titanium for strength and lightness. One of the major design criteria for Northrop was to build large carbon-fibre skins so as to ensure that the aircraft had as few openings as possible, which also helped to reduce radar returns. It was imperative that the number of access panels on the aircraft was kept to a minimum, as such seams can conspire to make the aircraft more visible. Northrop engineers, therefore, ensured that as much maintenance access could be obtained through essential openings such as the weapons and undercarriage bays and the flight deck doors. As far as the latter are concerned, their edges are serrated so as to make radar detection even more difficult.

One important thing to note is that stealth technology does not render an aircraft impossible to detect – it merely makes detection more difficult to achieve. The B-2A still has a radar signature, but the difference for this aircraft is that that radar signature is said to be just 0.64 square feet in size.

To this end, there has been a seemingly endless debate as to whether the B-2A can be detected by any kind of radar. A USAF document which was published in 1990 claimed that some powerful air defence radars could detect the jet, although it also acknowledged that in this eventuality, the aircraft 'could employ evasive routing, fly low to reduce coverage or use stand-off weapons to attack targets in the vicinity of those radars. Some of the larger-capable radars could detect the reduction from these radars long before the radar detects the bomber, and thus avoid the threat'.

Every effort has been made to ease the maintenance burden of the aircraft as much as possible. For instance, one of the jet's novel features is its self-diagnostic capabilities, which means that it can actually tell the maintenance crews what is wrong with it. Once a component on the aircraft fails, the flight control computer logs this and can subsequently produce a readout telling the maintainers which parts are not functioning. With some components, it is even possible for the B-2 to correct the fault while in flight.

This high level of automation means that the jet only requires two crewmembers. There was some initial debate as to whether the aircraft should have three personnel, including a navigator, and this was an objective

This photograph perfectly illustrates the rudderons at work on the aircraft. The Spirit's complex arrangement of control surfaces is essential for keeping what is an unstable design airborne. The workload for such a task is assumed by the aircraft's flight control computers and fly-by-wire systems (*USAF*)

Earth-bound KC-135Rs and a sky-bound B-2A during exercise *Northern Edge* 2002, which was hosted by Eielson AFB, Alaska (*SRA Walter Rodgers*)

SPIRIT OF KANSAS **touches down on the main runway at Eielson AFB whilst participating in the** *Northern Edge* **2002 training initiatives (***SRA Walter Rodgers***)**

of Gen John T Chain, who led SAC from 1986 until 1991. However, Gen Chain lost his battle and the aircraft would remain a two-crew platform – the USAF did allow some navigators to go through flight training to qualify as pilots on the aircraft. There are presently 300 USAF personnel and a single RAF officer (who benefited from an exchange programme with the 509th BW) who are qualified to fly the B-2A.

According to Col Eric Single, Vice Commander of the 509th BW, the lack of a third crewman brings its own challenges;

'The B-2 is a very pilot-friendly aeroplane in that capacity. It is pleasurable to fly because it does a lot of the work, and you get a lot of the information from the weapons system itself. Most of the complexities associated with flying it stem from its layout as a two-person jet. You don't have a bombardier, navigator or an electronic warfare officer, so both pilots are tasked with performing all of those additional duties as well. The automation of the aircraft's systems allows you to get all of that information and work it as a two-man crew without being task-saturated.'

The cockpit of the B-2A is not exactly spacious, both pilots sitting on an ACES II ejection seat which can get them out of the aircraft in a flash even when at zero speed and zero altitude. Tasks are divided between the Mission Commander, who sits in the left seat, and the Pilot, who sits on the right, although all crew members are trained to perform either task. In front of them is the aircraft's avionics panel. This is dominated by large six-inch colour displays. These were originally Cathode Ray Tubes, but they have since been replaced by more modern Liquid Crystal Multi-Function Displays. Surrounding each screen are the so-called 'bezzle' buttons which allow the crew to call up specific pages of information disclosing the status of the aircraft's systems, or its mission.

Like the B-1B, the aircraft is controlled by a stick rather than the yoke like the B-52. One of the key features of the aircraft's avionics is the Mission Recorder into which a pre-recorded 'tape' with information on the aircraft's mission can be fed into its computers. Should the B-2A be required to be 'retasked' while in flight, say because of new targeting priorities, new information on the mission can be keyed into the aircraft's mission computer. The cockpit of the aircraft is instantly recognisable because of its huge windscreens. These give excellent front and side views for the crew, and even have a fine wire mesh threaded through the glass to ensure that radar signals are blocked from entering the cockpit.

PERFORMANCE

There have been numerous reports stating that the B-2A is a nightmare to fly. However, this does not seem to be the case. The design is extremely 'clean', and the aircraft is said to be highly responsive to control inputs. One of the more challenging aspects to the aircraft is said to be conducting air-to-air refuelling, as the aircraft has a tendency to move forward when in the slipstream of a tanker, but careful management of the throttles mitigates this.

The aircraft is not known for being especially manoeuvrable, but this is arguably less of a consideration for a bomber than it would be for an air-superiority fighter. It is probably fair to say that the B-2A is the mid-way point in terms of the US bomber fleet when it comes to handling, certainly being more agile than a B-52H, but not in the league of the B-1B. Moreover, at low-level the B-1B is said to be more comfortable than the B-2A.

For most pilots, the shape of the aircraft does not make it behave particularly differently from any other large aircraft, and Northrop have more than compensated for its lack of vertical surfaces. For Lt Col Thomas Bussiere, CO of the 13th BS, 'there are unique characteristics of the B-2 that are not like any other aeroplane – obviously the design of it, the shape and the flight control inputs. For the operator, it's the same control column that is in other aircraft such as fighters. The pilot's inputs into the aircraft are traditional in nature, although the computers then translate them into the appropriate flight control inputs. So there's really nothing new to learn because the basics of aviation, and how to fly, are the same in this aeroplane as they are for almost any other'.

Lt Col Steve Basham, CO of the 393rd BS, agrees;

'It's a large aircraft, so it has a number of similarities. It rolls cleanly left and right. The jet has a great response to pitch inputs, so it's very responsive. The B-2 is not a light-your-hair-on-fire aircraft, but if you love technology and you want to put a bomb on target and be able to go anywhere in the world and utilise that stealth and sneak in and out and have that security, there's no better aircraft than the B-2.'

However, the B-2A departs from the behaviour of other more conventional aircraft when it is landing. The aircraft has a tendency to want to glide along when it gets into 'ground effect' – i.e. just above the ground, where the aircraft behaves as if it is floating along on a cushion of air and the pilots have to 'persuade' the jet to land through their control inputs. As Lt Col Basham noted, the FBW system helps in no small measure with this;

'There's a unique characteristic in this aircraft in that it does not have a vertical tail. Believe it or not, the computer in the aircraft actually senses the drift of the aircraft and puts in a force. When the aircraft lands, once the wheels compress it takes every bit of that out, so you actually feel a pretty good movement to the aircraft'.

Bussiere agrees saying that 'the aircraft is actually very easy to land. The hard part of the B-2 when landing is that you don't actually flare. That's why the comparison has been made between a B-2 landing and a carrier landing. Naval aviators don't flare either – they just drive into the flightdeck. The B-2 is unique in that aspect in the sense that as a big flying wing, as soon as the aircraft hits ground effect it wants to bunt up a little bit and carry on flying down the runway. When you hit ground effect, you feel it in the seat of your pants. The aircraft is very easy to land'.

In order to get to their targets, B-2 crews have several navigation systems at their disposal. The aircraft was fitted with a Navigational Sub System, which included both an Inertial Management Unit and the NAS-26 Astro-Inertial Unit – the latter works by using a telescope to fix the B-2A's position by observing the stars. There are a number of round plates to the left-hand side of the cockpit on the wing which house this system. Remarkably, the system works in daylight, provided that the bomber is at the right altitude. This equipment is also used alongside a trusty GPS system and a ring-laser gyro platform which allow the crew to ascertain the aircraft's exact position at all times.

For targeting, the aircraft was installed with the AN/APQ-181 radar, which was a descendent of the AN/APG-70 which was installed in the F-15E Strike Eagle. The system's electronically-steered array is located in the leading edge of each wing, and can be used for both navigation and targeting. Crucially, the radar has a 'low-probability of intercept' – in other words, it performs frequency-hoping and changes its pulsation patterns in order to disguise its signals from electronic 'background noise'. Apparently, much of the B-2A's radar technology stems from breakthroughs made during the *Tacit Blue* programme.

The cramped confines of the B-2A's cockpit, which is dominated by no fewer than eight 6-in Liquid Crystal Multi-Function Displays. Both crewmen are sat on ACES II zero-zero ejection seats (*Ted Carlson*)

All in all, the AN/APQ-181 radar has 21 operational modes. This allows crews to use a Synthetic Aperture Radar (SAR) which is essential for ground-mapping and accurate target identification, given that it provides a near-photographic quality representation of the target. Furthermore, this system is also capable of identifying moving ground targets – an echo back to the days of when the aircraft was earmarked with destroying mobile Soviet nuclear missiles. Facilities for weather-mapping and navigation are also installed, along with the ability to use the radar to aid air-to-air refuelling. Although ostensibly designed as a high-level platform, the aircraft can also use its radar for Terrain-Following/Terrain-Avoidance missions should a low-level flight to the target area be necessary.

During training, crews have to master all aspects of flying the aircraft. One particularly challenging procedure is refuelling, as the B-2 has a tendency to creep forward when in the slipstream of the larger KC-10 or KC-135. Here, *SPIRIT OF INDIANA* prepares to link up with a KC-10A (*Gary Ell*)

One of the most vital, and secret, items of equipment in the Spirit is the aircraft's Defensive Management Sub-System – the collection of electronics which help to mask the jet, and spoof any attempts by the enemy to lock either a radar or a missile onto it. What is known about the system is that its most important element is designated the AN/ZSR-63 Defensive Avionics Suite. It is thought that the system is able to actively cancel radar signals which are intercepted by the aircraft. Essentially, this works by emitting precisely the opposite electronic signal to that which is received, thus creating the electronic equivalent of white noise.

The B-2A is propelled by a total of four General Electric F118-GE-110 turbofans which keep the aircraft at a high-subsonic speed, given that they are not capable of re-heat. Each powerplant provides a total of 19,000 lbs of thrust, and they are buried deep within the wing, with two engines mounted side-by-side. Northrop also installed an Auxiliary Power Unit (APU) in the forward section of the left-engine mounting.

This allows the B-2 to start by itself, and to provide ground power for the aircraft's systems. The engines' performance is capable of taking the aircraft to altitudes of around 50,000 ft, with an unrefuelled range of around 6000 nautical miles. One visit to a tanker during a flight can take this range out to around 10,000 miles, with multiple refuelling extending the range therein.

Interestingly, the engines are invisible when viewing the aircraft from any angle. This is because fan blades have a habit of reflecting radar energy. Instead, they are fed with air through an 'S' bend which is lined with RAM to suitably distort any radar energy which enters the air intakes. Once the air has passed through the engine, it is then mixed with the airflow which passes over the wing to cool the exhaust, thus reducing the aircraft's infrared signature. Northrop also planned to install a system by which a chemical would have been added to the aircraft's exhaust to reduce the appearance of the contrail. This was abandoned, however, and instead a Laser-Radar-based system was installed to detect the contrail's formation and advise the pilot to descend to a lower altitude where the air would be warmer and the contrails' appearance thus less visible.

VARIANTS

The B-2A was produced in three variants. The initial aircraft delivered were in Block 10 configuration. This meant that they possessed a limited combat capability and could not launch conventional guided weapons. Block 10 aircraft were only able to drop either 2000-lb Mk 84 conventional gravity bombs or nuclear weapons. These aircraft were used primarily for training purposes.

Block 10 aircraft were followed by the Block 20 series. These jets possessed a modest ability to use conventional weapons, most notably the CBU-87/B Combined Effects Munition along with the Mk 84 bomb. These aircraft can also use gravity nuclear weapons.

The final series were Block 30 jets, seven of which were originally delivered, although all B-2As have now been upgraded to this status. These aircraft are vastly enhanced compared to their predecessors. Their radar modes are greatly improved, along with their terrain-following abilities. Block 30 jets are also able to deliver the Joint Direct Attack Munition (JDAM) and AGM-154A Joint Stand-Off Weapon (JSOW). They also fully conform to the aircraft's original radar signature requirements. Finally, their aft decks have been completely replaced and they have the full defensive avionics fit.

SPIRIT OF CALIFORNIA prepares for an evening sortie beneath a dramatic Missouri sunset. The aircraft's groundcrew have arrived in advance of the pilots, and they will soon being busy preparing the aircraft for its departure (*Ted Carlson*)

Keeping America's nuclear deterrent credible, even in the post-Cold War era, is a vital task, and regular exercises are held at Whiteman to ensure that B-2A Spirits can deliver a nuclear response if it was ever necessary. *SPIRIT OF HAWAII* taxies to the runway during one such exercise, known as the *Beast Walk* (*SRA Jessica Kochman*)

The aircraft's mission planning system is also more sophisticated, weapons management for Block 30 jets being provided via the aircraft's Generic Weapons Interface System (GWIS). The latter saw a digital software package installed that allowed the aircraft to carry an assortment of smart weapons for a single sortie. This meant that the B-2 was now capable of attacking four different targets during one mission. The transition to an all-Block 30 fleet began in July 1995, and was completed in 2000 when the last jet rotated through Northrop's Palmdale plant.

THE PUNCH

Each of the B-2A's two weapons bays is fitted with both a bomb rack and a rotary launcher which can be used for both nuclear and conventional weapons. The primary nuclear armament of the Spirit is the Mod-11 variant of the B61 free-fall nuclear bomb. This weapon has a hardened casing, is specifically designed to be used against reinforced targets and has a variable yield of between 10 and 340 kilotons (one kiloton is equivalent to 1000 tons of TNT).

The bomber is also capable of carrying the most powerful nuclear weapon in the USAF inventory, namely the B83 free-fall nuclear bomb. This weapon has a 1.2 megaton (one megaton is equivalent to one million tons of TNT) yield, and has been specifically designed to be delivered during low-level supersonic flight. It can also be used against hardened targets. Moreover, the weapon is optimised for airburst either with or without a parachute. Each weapon has been designed with a different mission in mind, and although both are capable of performing attacks against hardened targets, the B61-11 is the primary weapon in this respect, while the B83 is more suited to larger, more dispersed targets – an armoured formation of tanks for instance. The B-2A can deliver a total of 16 nuclear weapons in a single mission.

The other nuclear weapon compatible with the B-2A is the AGM-129 Advanced Cruise Missile, which is fitted with a W80 warhead and is specifically designed to evade enemy air defences and hit hardened targets. This weapon also has a variable yield of between 5 and 150 kilotons. Typically, a B-2A would be expected to carry around four B83s, 16 B61-11s or three AGM-129s during a nuclear mission.

There is some debate as to whether the B-2A would be used as a 'first strike' weapon during a nuclear conflict, given its relatively slow speed. It might instead be used to provide a second strike, or a retaliatory strike against an aggressor. It is perhaps for this reason that the B-2A can operate from relatively austere airfields, and can use any runway capable of accommodating a Boeing 727 airliner.

The B-2A remains a vital part of the Single Integrated Operations Plan (SIOP), which is at the heart of America's nuclear weapons doctrine, and which contains an array of war plans regarding how the United States would conduct nuclear combat. However, it is the Spirit's conventional capabilities which have come to the fore since the end of the Cold War.

The 'money-maker' for the aircraft is JDAM, 16 of which can be carried by the B-2A. These weapons have an unmatched capability against hardened targets ranging from command and control centres to weapons stores. Essentially, JDAM is an adaptor system which can fit onto most conventional bombs in the US arsenal. For the B-2A, the weapon best suited to JDAM upgrading is the 2000-lb Mk 84 general purpose unguided bomb, which is turned into a GBU-31 (the interim version was designated the GBU-36), or the 4700-lb BLU-113 hard-target penetrator, which becomes the GBU-37/B.

To give an insight into the bomber's punch when armed with JDAM, six B-2As could have executed Operation *Eldorado Canyon* against Libya in 1986. There air strikes required a total of 28 KC-10 and KC-135 tankers, five EF-111 Raven Electronic Counter-Measure (ECM) aircraft, 24 F-111 strike aircraft, 14 A-6E strike aircraft, 12 A-7E and F/A-18 aircraft providing ECM support, a brace of F-14 Tomcats and four E-2C Hawkeye command and control aircraft. Moreover, the B-2As could have performed their mission from CONUS without the need for European basing, and the political controversy that this caused.

For area targets, the aircraft can deploy the CBU-87 Combined Effects Munition (CEM). Each weapon contains 202 BLU-97/B bomblets, which can cover an area of 600,000 square feet . These submunitions can devastate light armour, equipment and personnel. A larger area munition is the CBU-89 Gator Mine, which contains 72 BLU 91/B anti-tank mines and 22 BLU-92/B antipersonnel mines. The destructive footprint caused by this weapon is 500,000 square feet.

Finally, the most modern area denial munition carried by the B-2A is the CBU-97 Sensor Fused Weapon, which boasts ten BLU-108/B submunitions containing four anti-armour weapons apiece. These are capable of detecting infrared targets and firing a shaped charge at them. The weapon's destructive footprint is around 650,000 square feet.

One of the most important conventional weapons to be cleared for use by the B-2A is Raytheon's JSOW, which can be launched up to 40 nautical miles from its target. The weapon uses both a GPS and Inertial Navigation System (INS), while infrared is used for terminal guidance to the target. JSOW is highly versatile, and can be fitted with an assortment of submunitions according to the mission. These can include BLU-97 bomblets for soft targets such as surface-to-air missile sites, or BLU-108 submunitions for hardened installations.

Looking to the future, the Spirit will also be modified to carry the Joint Air to Surface Stand-off Missile. This weapon can fly autonomously at low level in order to hit fixed and mobile targets. Moreover, it will fly its route in an indirect fashion in order to outfox air defences. This is possible thanks to its GPS-aided INS, which is highly jam-resistant.

THE PERSONNEL

There is a palpable *esprit de corps* among the personnel at Whiteman who work with the jet, thanks primarily to the demanding nature of the B-2A's mission. Lt Col Bussiere noted that, 'The proof in the pudding of any combat mission is the peacetime training. One of the things that the Air Force did very well is when we built the B-2 cadre, we didn't stick within the paradigm of the bomber community. We opened up the community to everyone, including the airlift community, and we brought in folks from all weapons systems in the Air Force to develop and mature the B-2.

'The fact that we have fighter, bomber, airlift and other support aircraft guys that have lent their experiences and made this weapons system what it is today is one of the strengths of the B-2 community.'

The security of secrecy – a trooper of the 509th Security Force stands guard over *SPIRIT OF ALASKA*. Anyone who has seen the B-2A on static display at an airshow will have seen a security presence around the Spirit which is almost as dramatic as the bomber itself. The guards are armed and will use their weapons if the situation requires (*TSgt Lance Cheung*)

An interesting size comparison between the two main aircraft types of the 509th BW. Parked side by side at an airshow, the *SPIRIT OF FLORIDA* appears to dwarf the T-38 Talon. However, both aircraft seem to be of a similar length! (*SSgt Bernard Wilson*)

Some of those at Whiteman have worked with the aircraft since it was still in the design and manufacturing phase. As such, there is a great fondness and loyalty for the bomber. Chief Master Sergeant Kelly Costa of the 509th Maintenance Group was full of praise for the Spirit;

'The aircraft's been a joy for me, having come from the B-52. The B-2 is just another aircraft in that sense, but the attributes it has, and its stealth, are fantastic.'

The maintenance of the aircraft can be time-consuming at times, but as Sgt Costa noted, it has also been a learning curve;

'Yes, it's a tedious aircraft because the low-observables take time to repair. Low-observables have come along way since when I first got here. The papers said that it couldn't fly through rain and that it couldn't do this and it couldn't do that. Of course people didn't realise that that aircraft was a toy from which we could learn, and now we've got a combat-ready aircraft that we've taken and proven three times.'

As a consequence, Sgt Costa and his colleagues are always busy;

'It is just another aircraft, but the uniqueness is the low-observables, so people talk about if we need this and if we need that. Sometimes we have to take care of the aircraft in a specific way because that is the nature of the beast. Actually, in terms of systems and basic hydraulics, I would say it's a better aircraft than others in the USAF inventory because it's newer. For example, our brakes last forever because they don't wear compared to those fitted to the B-52. Avionics is another area where the B-2 excels, as it's hard to compare the newer systems fitted in the jet with those in older aircraft. We have newer and different bugs which have not been worked out. Boeing and Northrop Grumman and all the companies which built the aircraft put a lot of work into the B-2, and it is a better aircraft maintenance-wise because of this.'

Chief Master Sergeant Beau Turner of the 509th Maintenance Group is similarly impressed by the development of LO maintenance knowledge that the B-2A has afforded to him and his colleagues;

'I equate this to the new model of a car. Ford, Chevy, Mercedes-Benz, whatever it might be, every year it gets better. As you find problems on older models of cars, you find improvements in the following years. With aircraft it is a little different, as you don't have a new and improved model year on year. Instead, you learn to cope with the areas which cause the most problems through decades of working on types such as the B-52 or B-1. Fixes adopted for these types are usually then applied as new maintainability and capability standards to more modern weapons systems such as the B-2.

'The lessons that we've learnt in the bomber community over the last two decades have been applied to the servicing of the B-2, and this in turn has meant that from a mechanical standpoint it is a very, very reliable aircraft. From an LO maintenance standpoint, a lot of the stuff which we are doing right now is at the leading edge of technology. We're learning every day to do things better, just as the contractors' are learning to provide us with better materials to keep the jet airworthy. Although the Air Force has two decades of knowledge gleaned from working with the F-117, about as close as that aircraft gets to the B-2 in terms of the technology it employs is the word "stealth"!'

Sgt Turner also recognises that the improvements to the aircraft as they have rotated through upgrades have also been a great help to the maintenance crews;

'I think that we have to talk about the evolutionary process of the B-2. First of all, the engineers would find components that don't fail as often. That's ideally what we want, and in a lot of cases the contractors' did a very good job. We are always looking for components which enhance the maintainability so that we don't have to break the skin to get into those areas to repair them. Now the Block 30 aircraft from an LO maintenance standpoint can be very tedious, as it requires meticulous work. You have a lot of different coatings and you have to remove a lot of stuff to get access to the panel covering the faulty part. Having carried out the work in the servicing bay, you then have to reinstall the panel and put all those LO materials back on. Every one of them requires some kind of curing process. That's a very time-consuming job.'

Col Single added that the B-2 also 'presents some of the same challenges found in other conventional aircraft. It's a heavy bomber, and it has multiple engines. The Low-Observables maintenance work that we do on it is a kind of a continual process. The maintainers have become very skilled at doing that. They devote a lot of time to maintaining the aircraft at a certain level of stealthiness, and we track that very closely so that we don't let aeroplanes get to a point where it would take a very long time to bring that back up to a pristine condition. That is something that we keep our eyes and hands on every day. The materials and the repair procedures have come a long way in the last ten years. We're much better either visually, or by using diagnostic tools, at taking a look at the jet and determining what anomalies are radar significant and what are not, and we keep track of repair times'.

The B-2A can also refuel from the KC-135, as seen here. During exercise *Northern Edge* 2002, the aircraft performed refuelling operations from both the Extender and the Stratotanker (*SRAD Myles Cullen*)

Although vastly different from the B-2, the T-38 is an invaluable training tool for the bomber crews. With sorties in the Spirit averaging just one or two per month, aircrew need to keep their flying hours up by conducting routine training hops in the Talons. Some 12 T-38As and two T-38Cs are assigned to the 394th CTS (*MSgt Keith Reed*)

The process of becoming a member of the B-2A team is very much a case of 'many being called, but few being chosen'. For the pilots, they must have a spotless flight record. No crews go straight onto the B-2A, and they will have already accrued experience in the fighter, bomber, airlift and support aircraft communities. Thousands of hours of flying experience and wing commander recommendation is essential. Quick learning skills and exposure to combat are also a great help.

Aircrew selection for the 509th BW is tough. Capt Adam 'Shift' Cuquet of the 394th CTS explained that 'quarterly, the Air Force holds a hiring board. To get to that hiring board you have to fill in an application. You have to fill out all the test scores which you have had from pilot training and all your big accomplishments throughout your career and submit all that to the board. They then look over how many applications there are and select maybe eight to ten people to actually interview – the number chosen usually depends on how many people they need and how many pilots they are bringing into the B-2 community.

'The interview consists of sitting down with different squadron commanders and with the wing commander. They ask you some questions, and you also perform a simulator flight so that they can evaluate your flying skills. When conducting the latter, they give you a couple of pages from the manual describing how to work some of the aircraft systems like the electronic displays. They will only give you a limited amount of information because they want to see your learning curve, to see how quick you are to pick things up. You spend about two days going to different interviews and talking to people, and you also do an aircraft tour. Then you go back to your base and a month later they publish who has been successful.'

For Capt Cuquet, who had flown B-1Bs prior to his arrival at Whiteman, notification of the success of his application was 'exciting, but it was a bittersweet thing because I love the B-1 community and I love the people in it. The B-2 has a more mature community which is definitely more top-heavy in rank. There are a lot more lieutenant colonels and full colonels, whereas the B-1 community is made up of more lieutenants and captains, with very few majors and lieutenant colonels. Obviously, going into the B-2 community was a challenge that I couldn't pass up'.

Once Capt Cuquet arrived at Whiteman, it was time to begin the training;

'Having joined the training squadron, the first step is to get flying again. The T-38 is used to get re-qualified, and after this you start your academics. The latter consists of three months of heavy academics before you actually start flying the B-2A. After that, you still continue with some academics, but you also start your flying. During the academic phase, you're taking tests, you're going to classes, but you're also working in different electronic mission trainers.'

These trainers include the Cockpit Procedures Trainer, which is specially designed to take students through the correct procedures for flying the aircraft. For example, if a student performs a particular procedure incorrectly, the simulator has to be reset and the student will perform the procedure again. The idea of this is to inculcate the student with the correct method of doing things on the flightdeck. During training in the simulator, every action which the pilot performs is electronically recorded. This means that the students can study their missions in acute detail once completed, and it also gives the instructors the chance to closely monitor their progress.

The last three months of the B-2 conversion course see pilots learning to fly the aircraft, and to use it as a weapons system. The final stage is for the crews to perform a mission qualification process, after which the pilot is certified to go into battle. Capt Cuquet noted that 'Once you're done with training, you get assigned to your bomb squadron, and that's where you get mission-qualified. When you go to the bomb squadron, you actually learn more about the jet's nuclear role. In the CTS, we teach some of the nuclear procedures, but we don't get the nuclear qualification. We still want to be just as sharp and on top of this strategic mission, despite our nuclear role having been toned down a little since the ending of the Cold War. We don't have a bomber in the sky night and day as we did then, for example'.

On average, pilots only fly one B-2A mission a week, with two training sorties usually flown back to back with the engines running during the crew change, removing the need to 'pre-fly' the aircraft a second time Around one in every five training flights sees a practice bomb drop of either a live or inert weapon at ranges in the Mid-West.

Before each flight, the crew will rehearse the sortie in the full-motion Weapon System Trainer (WST) simulator, which is said to have a 98 percent accuracy with the real thing. The simulator also accurately replicates the scenery around Whiteman within a 200-mile radius. The WST provides an invaluable tool via which missions can be rehearsed and prepared, as hostile territory and threats can be accurately simulated.

Given the *esprit de corps* at Whiteman, it is perhaps not surprising that the 509th BW does not have too many problems in terms of retention. Maj Gen Leroy Barnidge Jr, who was head of the 509th during Operation *Allied Force* in 1998, noted that 'I am blessed in some ways far greater than many of my fellow wing commanders. We don't have some of the retention problems that other bases are encountering. We are far above the Air Force average in terms of retention rates, and I think that is because people are actively trying to get into our B-2 programme. Therefore, they are here by personal choice. Once at Whiteman, they soon become exceedingly proud of what they are involved in. This pride permeates throughout the base. This is not reflective of many of the other installations around'.

A busy day in Missouri. *SPIRIT OF INDIANA* waits at the holding point for clearance to take-off while another aircraft lands at Whiteman (*MSgt Michael R Nixon*)

NOBLE ANVIL

In order to validate the 'Global Power' concept of deploying the B-2A, the 509th BW has to perform regular exercises away from its home base. Despite the fact that many recent operations involving the bomber have seen the aircraft flying direct to its targets from Whiteman, the wing has placed a major emphasis on being able to deploy and fight from Forward Operating Locations such as Andersen AFB, Guam. While it is possible for the aircraft to fight from CONUS, deploying the bomber closer to the action is sometimes preferable given that flight times to the target can be shorter. This can reduce wear and tear on the jets, which in turn increases availability, and a closer proximity allows more sorties to be generated.

With this in mind, two Spirits from the 509th BW deployed to Andersen AFB almost one year before Operation *Allied Force* got underway in March 1999. The exercise was intended to test every facet of what is necessary for B-2A forward operations. Usually, the bombers would be placed in the hangars at Andersen AFB. However, following Typhoon *Paca*, these hangars had sustained severe damage, forcing one of the aircraft to remain in the open at all times. The net effect of this was that the aircraft was either under strong tropical sunlight during the day or drenched with rain during tropical storms, which was about as much punishment as the aircraft's skin could be subjected to. In spite of this, the aircraft generated a 100 percent mission availability rate throughout the entire period of the exercise, accumulating almost 90 flying hours before returning to CONUS.

This mission to Guam was followed up by a second later in the year, which saw three aircraft deployed with the 2nd Expeditionary Group – three B-52Hs were also involved. The aircraft deployed from their bases at Whiteman and Barksdale, in Louisiana, respectively for a 'Global Power' training mission. Col Bob Bruley of the 2nd Expeditionary Group recalled, 'We did exactly what we said we were going to do when we first arrived. We deployed to a Forward Operating Location (FOL) and proved to the world

The extraordinary characteristics of the B-2 mean that a high premium is placed upon mission planning prior to a training flight or combat. The goal is to get things right the first time, and to thoroughly calculate and comprehend the risks to the aircraft as much as possible before the sortie is flown. To this end, Majs Scott Land and Jim Smithers look over a flight plan map as they prepare for a mission (*MSgt Rose S Reynolds*)

A dramatic sky at Nellis AFB during a *Red Flag* exercise provides the backdrop for two B-2s. *SPIRIT OF ALASKA*, in the foreground, prepares to taxi towards the runway in preparation for a night training mission (*MSgt Michael R Nixon*)

that we could conduct training missions within the Pacific theatre'. Missions took the jets as far north as South Korea and as far south as Wake Island.

Since the 509th BW attained full operational capability with the B-2 on 1 April 1997, it has constantly maintained SIOP readiness in the event of a nuclear war. To this end, the B-2's nuclear capabilities have been tested and evaluated at regular intervals. One year before the aircraft was flying over Serbia, a B-2A performed flight tests with B61-11 inert nuclear weapons at Eielson AFB, Alaska. As part of the tests, on 26 March 1998 a Spirit dropped two B61-11 shells on the Stuart Creek Impact Area to test the weapon's ground penetration characteristics – the bomb is designed to destroy high-value, deeply-buried targets. The choice of location was especially pertinent, given the frozen soil of the impact area.

Importantly, the tests were also performed to ensure that the weapon's internal components remained intact so that they could explode once they had penetrated the earth. The net result was that the weapon succeeded in burrowing through ten feet of earth.

Despite the original B61 bombs having entered the US arsenal in the 1960s, the weapon underwent significant modifications in its B61-11 guise, which was designed to allow the weapon to penetrate up to 25 ft of ground before exploding. In order to make the test as realistic as possible, short of performing an atmospheric detonation of a nuclear bomb, the internal components of the weapon were constructed from depleted uranium, which is said to closely mirror the physical characteristics of the weapons-grade material which would usually be found in the B61-11.

SPIRIT GOES TO WAR

'If there is ever another war in Europe, it will come out of some damned silly thing in the Balkans' prophetically warned the nineteenth-century German statesman Otto von Bismarck. Ethnic strife, ethnic cleansing and civil war had festered in the ashes of Yugoslavia for most of the 1990s, following the end of the Cold War and the break-up of the country. An intervention by NATO against the Bosnian Serb forces which were laying siege to Sarajevo (the capital of Bosnia-Herzegovina) in the form of air strikes during Operation *Deliberate Force* in 1995 was sufficient to bring a momentary and uneasy peace to this troubled region. It would, however, remain as a temporary measure.

Serbian President Slobodan Milosevic seemed bent on a showdown with the West, and in 1998 fighting erupted between the Serbian armed forces and the so-called Kosovo Liberation Army (KLA), which was

An MB-2 towing tractor pushes *SPIRIT OF WASHINGTON* into its hangar at Whiteman ready for post-flight maintenance checks, having completed a sortie on Day 30 of OAF. The bomber proved to be an indispensable arrow in NATO's quiver over Serbia (*SSgt Michael Gaddis*)

attempting to unite all ethnic Albanians in the province of Kosovo and the Former Yugoslav Republic of Macedonia into a greater Albania. The result was the commencement of the forcible expulsion of the Kosovar Albanian population from the province by the Serbian security apparatus.

The US-led Western bloc of nations was emphatic that it would not sit around and watch on this occasion, as yet another of Milosevic's ethnic cleansing forays began. Despite a mission by the Organisation for Security and Cooperation in Europe over the winter months of 1998 to verify that a shaky cease-fire was enduring in the province, the situation deteriorated in January 1999, when violence between the KLA and the Serbian Army and Special Police units resumed.

Peace talks involving NATO, the Serbian government and the KLA held at Rambouillet, outside Paris, broke up on 19 March when the Serbian delegation refused to accept a settlement. The stage was now set for NATO to embark upon Operation *Allied Force* (OAF) – an air campaign that saw the largest number of assets contributed by the United States under the codename Operation *Noble Anvil* (ONA).

The objective of the OAF air campaign was to 'Ensure a verifiable stop to all military action and the immediate ending of violence and repression in Kosovo; withdrawal from Kosovo of Serbian military, police and para-military forces; agreement to the stationing in Kosovo of an international military presence; agreement to the unconditional and safe return of all refugees and displaced persons, and unhindered access to them by humanitarian organisations; and to provide credible assurance of Serbian willingness to work on the basis of the Rambouillet Accords in the establishment of a political framework agreement for Kosovo in conformity with international law and order and the Charter of the United Nations'.

OAF was to be the debut of the Clinton doctrine of foreign policy, which would see the United States attempting to manage conflicts in failed states and, according to Leslie Gelb, President of the Council of Foreign Relations, 'wars of national debilitation, a steady run of uncivil civil wars sundering fragile but functioning nation states'. This conflict also gave a combat debut to a plethora of high and low-cost advanced US weapons systems. The expensive Boeing C-17 Globemaster III freighter and the thrifty GPS-Aided Munition (GAMs), the precursor to the GBU-31 satellite-guided JDAM, being but two, with the latter being dropped by that other debutant, the B-2A Spirit.

MAKING THE COMMITMENT

When OAF commenced the Spirit had not long been in service, and it was, along with its B-52H cousin, one-half of the USAF's segment of America's nuclear deterrent. Yet the Kosovo war would give the jet an important opportunity. While the use of nuclear weapons was out of the question, the B-2's impressive bomb load could put a substantial quantity of 'iron-on-target' in Serbia. But that was not all. Serbia had one of the most sophisticated air defence systems in the world. Bombing the country was going to be extremely hazardous for Allied aircrews – so much so that they were ordered to maintain a strict minimum height of 15,000 ft during the first half of the campaign until Serbian air defences were judged to be sufficiently degraded to permit operations at a lower altitude.

The B-2, however, had been designed with such sophisticated air defences in mind. It was time to see whether the American taxpayers' cash had paid off, and whether the Spirit would 'do exactly what it said on the tin'. Moreover, the ability to separately target 16 different aim points with 16 different GAMs would almost certainly give the Serbian military and government something to think about. But this was not all. The aircraft only put two crewmembers at risk during the operations, as opposed to the scores of aircrew which would be required for a conventional strike package of non-stealthy aircraft flying straight into the Serbian hornet's nest on 'Night One' of the action.

There was just one catch – Whiteman AFB, tucked away in the middle of Missouri, was about as far away from the Balkans as possible. Any flights to and from the base would be exhaustive, super-long haul sorties during which the crews would need to stay alert and 'on message' at all times. It was said that the sortie times were the first and most immediate concerns of the pilots.

For those working at Whiteman, it was no foregone conclusion that the B-2A would participate until right before show-time on 24 March 1999. Sgt Turner remembers ONA vividly;

'*Allied Force* to us was a pretty big deal. It was all classified, but we knew our jets were going. We'd been watching the news. We knew that the pilots were going to come back home, and that we were going to strike the targets that we needed to strike – remember, we didn't just go after everything and anything. We went after heavily defended, hardened targets. That's our job. There were a lot of folks counting on us. When you're doing that from the CONUS, that's a pretty big deal, as one day the aviator is in an aeroplane over the target and 24 hours later he's back at home cutting his grass! OAF was a big deal because it was the first time that we entered combat. We expected losses to Serbian defences, but instead we had great success.'

Some members of the B-2 community had commented that the commitment of the jet to combat operations had been in the pipeline since 1997, but had always come to nothing. This constant official 'crying wolf' on the aircraft's involvement had led to a certain degree of scepticism in some quarters of the B-2A world as to whether the aircraft would ever actually participate in combat. When news reached Whiteman that the 509th BW might be getting involved in ONA, there was every expectation that the unit might again be stood down, as it had been during Operation *Desert Fox*, when targets had been bombed in Iraq in December 1998. Two weeks prior to the commencement of hostilities it looked almost certain that the B-2A would be joining the action as the very first Allied aircraft to arrive in the skies of Serbia.

During OAF, a total of nine operational B-2As were available to the 509th BW on the ramp at Whiteman AFB. Eight of these aircraft were assigned to combat, with a single jet kept as an operational reserve. Those B-2As not available were far from idle, as new pilots still needed to be trained. These jets were also kept busy with the Spirit's continuing operational evaluation programme.

The pilots chosen to fly the aircraft during the early combat missions were the most experienced crews at Whiteman at the time. However, by the end of the campaign, the frequency with which the B-2A had been used meant that nearly all of the qualified Spirit pilots in the 509th BW

Another photograph of *SPIRIT OF WASHINGTON* being returned to its hangar at Whiteman in the aftermath of a marathon OAF mission. The analysis of the aircraft's performance and condition after a sortie was imperative to ensuring that problems with the bomber could be identified early so as to ensure that it was not prevented from participating in future sorties. Such analysis immediately post-mission was crucial when it came to ensuring the availability of the six B-2As committed to OAF (*SSgt Michael Gaddis*)

had seen combat. However, the decision to rotate as many B-2A pilots as possible through the war-torn skies of Serbia was not taken at the beginning of the campaign.

Planners at the 509th BW initially thought that ONA would run for a fraction of the 78 days that it would end up taking, and that Milosevic would be persuaded to conclude his actions in Kosovo once Allied weaponry had destroyed his key military targets. As it was, OAF would run for almost three months. The rotation of aircrews became necessary, not only to give all pilots combat experience, but also to ensure that stealth bomber operations could continue smoothly with fresh crews. The Air Force did not want to place undue pressure on those who had flown the initial strikes. There was a belief among the 509th leadership that spreading the combat experience amongst as many crews as possible would be of benefit in the future, and as operations in Afghanistan and Iraq later illustrated, this decision handsomely paid off.

The issue of flight times would dominate the debate over the B-2A's deployment to OAF. There were discussions in the Pentagon as to whether the aircraft should forward-deploy to Europe in much the same way as their B-1B and B-52H bomber brethren had done. As it was, the sortie demands placed on the 509th BW by Supreme Commander Europe, Army Gen Wesley K Clark, meant that CONUS basing for the aircraft was feasible.

Had Gen Clark required more sorties, forward basing may have become a more pressing issue, and even a necessity. The net effect of not forward basing the B-2As was two-fold. Firstly, the heightened security which would have had to accompany a B-2A deployment to Europe was one less thing for the 509th BW to worry about. Secondly, the airlift that a stealth bomber deployment would have necessitated to Europe in terms of spare parts, equipment and personnel meant that USAF airlift assets, which are always in high demand and in short supply, could be allotted to other tasks.

One 'halfway-house' in the debate was the so-called 'employ-deploy' option. The idea was for the B-2As to take off from Whiteman, fly to their targets in the Balkans, drop their ordnance and recover to a base in Europe – almost certainly RAF Fairford in Gloucestershire, England, where the B-1Bs and B-52Hs were operating from. Once there, the aircraft could be rearmed for a new mission, fly back to the Balkans, drop its bombs and then return to Whiteman. It was thought that 'employ-deploy' would give the best of both worlds, achieving more sorties without actually having to move the support infrastructure.

Weaponry was another consideration. During OAF, the B-2A would be the only platform to deliver the new GBU-31 JDAM. At the start of the campaign, there were around 600 JDAM in US stocks – the only country to use the weapon. As luck would have it, Boeing's GAM factory is just up the road from Whiteman at St Charles, Missouri. All the GAMs were already at Whiteman prior to the commencement of hostilities. Moving the aircraft overseas meant that their bombs would have to go too, along with any additional units which Boeing would build in the meantime.

Despite the prevailing feeling of 'go/no-go' for the staff at White-

man, planning for the B-2A's employment in operations against Serbia began weeks in advance of the aircraft's initial strikes on 24 March. The fixed, heavily defended military targets which the bomber would go after had already been identified and were programmed into the B-2A's simulators at Whiteman to allow crews to begin practising their strikes. By the time that actual combat missions were being flown, they had already been rehearsed many times in the simulator.

Given that the smallest amount of time possible would be spent over the target area, it was possible to practise the bomb run and weapons release several times in the simulator during a single day in order to perfect the mission. Pilots would also practise missions based on threat data which had been collected by the bomber during previous sorties in order to simulate these flights as accurately as possible. This, combined with the airmanship of the crews, the hard work of those on the ground and the sophistication of the B-2A weapons system gave the bomber an extremely impressive kill rate.

The simulator flights saw every aspect of the mission being rehearsed. Crews tried to work through all possible problems that they might face, deciding on a course of action to be taken should something go wrong. Meanwhile, hard at work, in an isolated corner of the base, protected behind reams of barbed-wire and security systems, the B-2A Mission Planning Cell meticulously orchestrated every aspect of the mission.

It is said that the Mission Planning Cell has the world's most comprehensive database on global air defence capabilities – a vital part of ensuring that the B-2A can go about its tasks undisturbed. The Mission Planning Cell performs a vital role,

'No one kicks ass without tanker gas' is the popular refrain of USAF refuelling crews, and the B-2A is no exception. While the Spirit has an enviable range, flying from Whiteman to the Balkans unaided would have run the tanks dry. Not since the RAF's *Black Buck* raids during the Falklands War of 1982 had such sorties been mounted. Here, 88-0330 of the 325th BS replenishes its tanks prior to entering battle (*USAF*)

SPIRIT OF MISSISSIPPI is readied for a mission over the former Yugoslavia. On the bomb trolley sits four GAMs – the B-2's weapon of choice for the conflict (*SRA Jessica Kochman*)

given that the aircraft is not 'invisible' to radar in the true sense of the word – it is extremely difficult to detect, however. Because of this, prior to a sortie being flown, the aircraft's capabilities have to be cross-referenced with the potential threats that it will face so as to ensure that the B-2 can indeed perform the mission without getting shot down.

According to Col Single, 'Our intelligence community routinely tracks and tries to keep up with all the different changes to the air defence capabilities throughout the world, and that's just one of their primary duties. All assets are very concerned about having the most current order of battle possible. We emphasise that the pilots on all missions – even short ones – spend a lot of time planning their flight so that they don't experience too many surprises during a sortie. Such planning also allows them to know when their high-path critical loading is going to occur so that they can work around it. One of the things that we brief are "crunch points" – those parts of the mission when you know that task-loading is going to increase, so you try to de-conflict those and prepare yourself as best you can.'

INTO BATTLE

By 20 March 1999, the targets for the first night's operations had already been allocated, and the crews were studying their missions. It also appears that the pilots had received their GPS targeting coordinates that the B-2s and GAMs would use to locate and destroy their targets. Finally, they had been given imagery of the target area which they could check against the imagery returned from the aircraft's SAR. With all this information to hand, it was the crew's job to write the aircraft's flight plan. This would include planning for air-to-air refuelling, and also navigating a safe path through Serbian air defences. Around 36 hours before the first two B-2As took off for their targets, the bomber crews started to get some rest ahead of the marathon missions that they would fly.

For the American public, and for the wider world, the murmurings that the Spirit would be used over Serbia would soon become shouts. The advent of satellite news broadcasting meant that speculation over the B-2A's use was beamed around the world in near real-time as the Kosovo crisis unfolded. Such news would not be lost on the Serbian leadership. While this had a psychological impact, leaving Milosevic and his cronies in no doubt that America's most potent airborne weapons system was about to be unleashed against them, there has been speculation that TV transmissions of the jet taking off might have also given the regime a rough warning time as to when they could expect the bomber to strike. However, this has been disputed.

While the crisis was developing, the 509th BW continued its usual cycles of training flights and base operations. How it would have been possible to distinguish a B-2A taking off for a training flight or for a combat mission is anybody's guess, particularly as the aircraft does not carry its ordnance externally.

The culmination of almost two decades of development, billions of dollars of taxpayers' money and at times highly acrimonious political and media debate was about to be put to the test. The entire gestation of the B-2A had seen numerous, and often uninformed comments regarding what the aircraft could and could not do. Editorial inches were occupied by leader writers telling the world that this horribly expensive jet could not fly through rain, could be tracked by rudimentary battlefield air defence systems, would not fly without legions of supporting aircraft because of its high value and would not even be committed to combat because the aircraft was just too expensive and important to be put at risk. All of this was proved to be resoundingly incorrect.

For Lt Col Bussiere the first night was an anxious time;

'I was the Operations Officer of the 325th BS at the time. It was the only squadron that we had here at Whiteman then. We performed the mission requested of us, despite many people having apprehensions about whether the aircraft would survive in combat, and whether or not the stealth thing really worked. I can tell you that the folks who actually executed the mission had 110 percent confidence in the B-2, and there wasn't any apprehension amongst the crew members as they stepped out the door for the first time to go fly combat in the aircraft. There may have been other folks in the Air Force, the US government or in the world that had their doubts cleared or their apprehensions eased following this mission, but I can tell you that all of us at Whiteman never really had a doubt that our brothers would be coming back from combat.'

Five hours before take-off, the crews returned to the base from their mandatory pre-mission rest, were briefed on their missions and were strapped into their aircraft.

'Typically, you'll come in and you'll get a pre-mission briefing from your Intel folks. You'll study your administrative portion of your briefing. You'll sign out your life support gear. You'll get all suited-up. If it's a long duration mission, we may or may not have a pre-flight crew who go out there and pre-flight the jet for you so you don't spend as much time on the ground as you would do normally, and then you basically fly the mission', remembers Lt Col Bussiere.

Rest planning was a vital part of mission preparation. The B-2As would take off for their targets at night, and also drop their ordnance at night. Effectively, the B-2A crews would have to be at their most alert and their most active at a time when the human body feels that it should be resting.

After the false alarms, adrenaline and anti-climaxes, the Spirit finally went into battle in the early hours of 24 March 1999 – two years after the aircraft had achieved Initial Operating Capability. Two B-2As, each loaded with 16 GAMs, launched from Whiteman and headed for the Balkans. Their attacks followed air and sea-launched missiles fired earlier – they were the first manned aircraft to fly over their targets.

Lt Col Basham was one of those crewmembers who flew on the first two B-2A strikes into Serbia. He remembers the atmosphere at Whiteman;

'On that first one, we'd been building up so many times. If you go back to ONA, we were told that it was on and then it was off. Literally, every night we were coming in and our bodies were on the cycle. We were ready to go. As we took off for that first mission, there was just a very slight surreal moment when we looked at each other and said "I can't believe that we're going". Finally, we actually made it airborne, but from that moment on it was all business.'

When operating in pairs, the bombers would usually fly together from Whiteman across the Atlantic, even if they were striking different targets. During the outward leg, the aircraft would usually perform three refuelling operations in total – two as they traversed the Atlantic and one

37

in the Mediterranean just prior to entering the combat area. The flight to Serbia would see the crews constantly reviewing aspects of the mission. They would study target imagery and recheck the status of the B-2. Weather reports and updates would also be supplied to the crew. These updates, coupled with mission planning and rehearsal, was intended to make sure that the jet performed its mission perfectly first time.

Lt Col Basham and his colleagues would be the first manned aircraft to fly into Serbia, and they would be doing this alone against some of the most heavily defended targets in the world;

'When you're going in-country, and you're waiting for that first sign that something is going on, it is all business. You're focused on the mission at hand because so many people have just poured their hearts into this, even if we go back to Jack Northrop himself. Of course he was not with us, but to go into combat for the first time would have been a dream for him. To be able to take that aircraft in, you know that you are delivering what many people have put together. These thoughts are not in your mind at the time, however, because to you the mission is all business – you're focused on the point at hand.'

Once airborne, one of the biggest challenges for the crew was getting rest. In order to make sure that the pilots were at their maximum efficiency, they would sleep in shifts, and it was imperative for each crew member to get precisely the correct amount of sleep. Too much sleep and the pilot will awaken tired, too little and the pilot will still be fatigued. Strict adherence to meal times would also go some way into assisting the pilots' alertness. One of the most challenging aspects to a pilot getting enough sleep is the B-2's small cockpit. Lt Col Basham recalled;

'We actually have less room inside the B-2 than we do inside of a B-1. For those long sorties you have got to decide what you're going to do when you get out of your seat. If you get out of your seat to take a nap, you have a cot that fits in the small space that we have. But if you have the cot down, you're not going to be able to stand in that space. If you have the cot stowed away, you can stand there. Those are all just small items, but it's a tight cockpit.'

Fortunately the cot, which was said to have been purchased from a local store down the road from Whiteman, was a perfect fit for the cockpit.

Col Single explained that considerable effort had gone into ensuring that the aircrews would remain alert when necessary;

'We did a lot of work with Human Engineers in the early days of the B-2. We train our aircrews on long duration abilities. One of the training requirements we do before they are qualified is to perform a long-duration simulator mission, and we keep them in the "sim" for up to 24 hours – we even had someone go for almost 50 hours! We did a lot of work with Human Engineers, who would monitor your pulse rate when you were sleeping and when you were not on the simulator missions. Thanks to their data, we have been able to train pilots with proper diets and exercise regimes. We actually build specific meal profiles into the sortie, and schedule nap time to allow one of the pilots to get out of the seat for a fairly extended time so as to get crew rest between flight activities.'

Interestingly, during the operations against Serbia, the B-2As, as a general rule, did not operate with other assets as part of a strike package, but instead performed their missions either as singletons or in pairs outside of the NATO command. They were often utilised to perform the opening strikes as part of a larger air assault, much as their F-117A Nighthawk cousins had done on the opening night of Operation *Desert Storm* seven years earlier. Their arrival and departure times from Serbian airspace were very carefully scripted.

It is important to note that on occasions, the B-2As in-theatre did take advantage of support from electronic warfare aircraft such as the US Marine Corps' Italy-based EA-6B Prowlers. Those close to the B-2A community insist that this was done not because the jet's low observable characteristics were insufficient, but because 509th BW mission planners wanted to give their crews as much protection as they possibly could.

Moreover, despite the autonomous nature of B-2A operations during OAF, a Spirit pilot was placed with the planning staff of Lt Gen Michael C Short, Allied Air Forces Southern Europe Commander at the NATO Combined Air Operations Centre (CAOC) at Vincenza, Italy. This was not only done to ensure that CAOC leaders were fully aware of the bomber's capabilities, but also to provide a subtle degree of lobbying regarding the part that the bomber could play in the air war.

As they prepared to enter hostile airspace, the crews got themselves ready for combat. They suited-up once again in thermal underwear, winter flight jackets and a life vest, aware of the cold temperatures of the Balkans and the Mediterranean Sea beneath them. After this, the weapons were checked, as was the datalink from the aircraft's mission computer to the bombs.

As the jet approached its aim point, its SAR would take a picture of the target. The detail revealed by these pictures is legendary, and taking a 'picture' is a particularly accurate description. This SAR photo was then matched with the overhead imagery of the target which was provided to the crews to verify that they were about to attack the correct target. Once this process was complete, the target's GPS coordinates were verified via the B-2A's GPS-Aided Targeting System (GATS). The GATS is a weather-beating system allowing the crews to double-check the position of their target and the bomb aim points even in inclement weather.

Any necessary updating of the coordinates would then take place, these in turn being fed into the bomb's guidance system. This could be done by steering the cursor on the SAR to the desired point of impact and then designating it. This would produce a precise GPS coordinate which was then dialled into the weapon if any changes were necessary. As the target was approached, the bomb-bay doors would open at the last possible moment (in order to conceal the aircraft's radar signature for as long as possible) and the weapons would be dropped clear of the B-2, before steering themselves towards the target. Generally, the aircraft would drop eight weapons in each single pass. On some occasions the bomber even dropped 16 separate GAMs on 16 different targets.

One pilot flying during ONA noted that when the bomb doors opened, the Spirit would slightly decelerate, and there would be a slight jolt as the weapons were released. Apart from this, the crews would feel nothing. The jet remained very stable throughout the entire procedure, apart from the pilots needing to throttle forward slightly to maintain the aircraft's speed.

The flight times to the Balkans usually took about 15 hours, while five hours were spent loitering outside the combat area. The flight back to

Whiteman lasted another 13 hours. Once the attack was complete, the aircraft would then perform two more refuelling operations on its way back to the CONUS. After arrival at Whiteman, the aircraft would be thoroughly checked over by the groundcrews, before being readied to fly once more. For the pilots, it would be time for some rest, before getting back into the rotation for another mission.

It was on the B-2's return leg to Missouri that the nation and the world began to wake up to the feat that the bomber had just accomplished. Lt Col Basham remembers that 'when we came back into the country the next morning – and by the way we flew past two more B-2s that were headed east – we were able to quickly bring them up on the radio. We talked to New York Center (air traffic control), who are the first folks that you'll talk to depending on from where you came in. They knew who we were and where we'd been. You could tell the pride in their voices that they were welcoming home a couple of folks that maybe had made history, but more so had taken the fight to someone else, and shown the pride of a nation and the jet's capability.'

B-2As would not just go after the hard and well-defended targets. The way in which the aircraft was utilised was fascinating. On one occasion, a Spirit was tasked with attacking the intersection of two runways on a Serbian airfield. The bomber placed a number of GAMs directly onto the intersection, producing large craters which effectively put both runways out of commission. This attack had the added value of preventing the Serbian aircraft at the base from taking off either to escape, harass Allied aircraft or to participate in the ground war against the KLA. Once grounded, these aircraft were easy pickings for the other non-stealthy jets which followed the B-2A raid on the base. The airfield was duly pummelled by B-1Bs and B-52Hs, which dropped unguided bombs. This particular B-2 actually hit two airfields during the course of this mission.

In an incident reminiscent of the Thanh Hoa bridge in North Vietnam, which survived 800 sorties generated by US warplanes, the Novi Sad combined railway and highway bridge in northern Serbia would just not collapse. Prior to the B-2A's visit, an F-15E had placed two GBU-15 2510-lb TV-guided bombs onto its spans, but to little effect. More metal was then used in the form of two 2000-lb BLU-109A/B 'Have Void' penetrator weapons, dropped from an F-117A, but these failed too. Finally, a Spirit was called in. It dropped six GAMs into a 1600-square foot area on the central span of the bridge, before placing two weapons on the northern span. The result? No more bridge! Other targets to receive the B-2's attention included the Kragjevic armament factory and the Crvena Zastava vehicle plant in central Serbia.

For the most part, data on the targets which the B-2A attacked is still highly classified, and for good mea-

They had always said that Yugoslav President Josip Broz Tito made the trains run on time, but this would become much more difficult for his Serbian successor Slobodan Milosevic, especially when a B-2A Spirit dropped the Novi Sad combined railway and road bridge after it had withstood several assaults by other USAF aircraft (*NATO*)

NOVI SAD RAILROAD & HWY BRIDGE OVER DANUBE, SERBIA
PRE STRIKE | POST STRIKE

sure. Betraying the exact nature of the targets destroyed could encourage potential adversaries to fortify similar installations still further prior to a confrontation with the United States. This is highly significant given that the B-2A plays a vital role in destroying the nerve centres of air defence command and control installations in preparation for follow-on waves of non-stealthy aircraft. Failure to neutralise such objectives can at best severely hamper an air campaign and at worst render it all but impossible to prosecute. What we do know is that on the very first night, the B-2As went into business against heavily-defended Serbian air defence targets. Throughout the campaign, the bomber targeted the SA-3 (NATO codename 'Goa') surface-to-air missile systems and their accompanying radar systems.

Other targets included secure facilities such as command and control installations and communications sites. So called 'infrastructural' elements were also included, such as military production facilities and bridges. It would not be unrealistic to assume that the B-2A was chosen for the latter targets for two reasons – its large bomb load and ability to operate over Serbia in a comparatively high-threat environment. For example, the military production factory might not have been a hard target in the true sense of the word, but it was probably protected by a thick screen of air defences impregnable to a non-stealthy aircraft.

One of the targets hit by the B-2 resulted in OAF's biggest diplomatic *faux pas* when, on 7 May, the Chinese Embassy in central Belgrade was hit by three GAMs. Three people were killed and the incident unleashed a barrage of noisy protests from the Chinese government. No sooner had tempers flared than the conspiracy theorists began to work overtime, speculating on why the Embassy had been attacked. 'Cloak and Dagger' tales of the Chinese government providing a secret communications conduit for Serbian government radio transmissions to their forces in the field was one of the milder theories posted on the internet. The reality may well have been far less exciting.

It seems that the US government's Central Intelligence Agency had used an out-of-date map for targeting, having thought that the building was the Serbian Federal Directorate for Supply and Procurement. The 509th BW was completely in the clear. It had been issued with targeting coordinates and imagery and had attacked the target as ordered. Responsibility for the error lay far further up the chain of command with the CIA and, ultimately, with President Bill Clinton.

So successful was the GAM/Spirit 'double-whammy' that by 1 April, the USAF had used up 224 of the weapons – more than one-third of its total stock. This illustrates that up to this point in ONA the B-2As had flown 14 individual aircraft sorties, averaging at least one B-2A single-ship sortie per day. The jets' appetite for these weapons was fast becoming insatiable, causing the DoD to issue an order for a further 5410 guidance kits which could be attached to either Mk 84 dumb bombs or BLU-109A/B weapons in order to create the GAM package.

Between 5 and 12 April, the aircraft expended a further 162 GAMs, and on these occasions the B-2s were mostly performing dual-ship missions.

CONCLUSIONS

Several lessons were learnt from the B-2A deployment during OAF, but one of the most important, according to the groundcrews, was that the

41

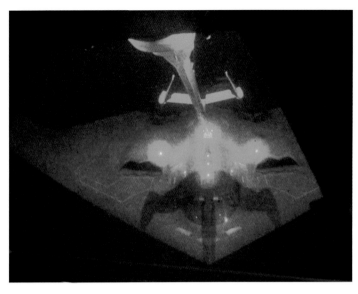

aircraft required far less maintenance than they had initially expected. During one instance, the ground-crews had managed to turn a jet around within four hours of landing, while on another occasion, the interval between landing and the next sortie was four days! The main factor slowing the maintenance down was not necessarily the complex and intricate replacement of delicate systems, but instead the curing time needed for the LO materials and paints which had to be reapplied to an aircraft after a mission. One source said that the curing time for damaged LO materials was one day per mission flown by the B-2.

A B-2A makes its way home to Missouri after attacking targets in Serbia. The tanker effort was crucial to the Spirit's mission success in OAF, crews having to refuel in the dead of night. This photo was taken through Night Vision Goggles (*USAF*)

The major failure item on the aircraft throughout OAF was the Actuator Remote Terminal (ART), which controlled the aircraft's surfaces, and without which the B-2A cannot fly. An airflow cooling problem on the aircraft had caused the ART to become a high-failure item during the campaign. However, the difficulties experienced by the B-2 were not sufficient to ground the bombers, and despite a shortage in the supply of spare parts, the ART system could still be repaired.

To summarise, the aircraft retained a mission-capable rate of 75 percent – a figure which did not include LO-material maintenance. When LO repair and replacement was taken into account, the figure dropped to 65 percent mission availability rate. Despite this, all B-2A sorties began on time, and only a single aircraft aborted its mission because of mechanical problems. One aircraft landed back at Whiteman for repairs, and was turned around in

Almost home, a B-2A takes fuel from a KC-135 over the CONUS during the final stages of yet another Serbian sortie (*USAF*)

15 minutes before being sent on its way. Two other missions were cancelled because NATO had political misgivings about the intended targets.

The rest period for the pilots started three days prior to the mission being flown. Speaking on 25 March 1999, Col Tony Imondi, who was the 509th BW's Operations Group Commander at the time , noted that 'The B-2 was designed to deliver weapons on the first day – yesterday was the first day of the war, and the B-2 was there'. The general consensus amongst the 509th BW leadership was that the aircraft was able to accomplish its required tasking with very few problems. Interestingly, this was being done while the jet continued to be maintained on nuclear deterrent alert under the SIOP. OAF showed that the aircraft carried equal weight as both a conventional and nuclear bomber.

Another important 'selling point' for the aircraft was its ability to drop weaponry in any and all weathers. Bad weather plagued OAF, and on occasions caused major headaches for NATO aircrew as they sought to attack Serbian targets while striving to keep collateral damage to a minimum. On one occasion, the entire air war planned for a particular evening was scrubbed when it became clear that the weather would prove to be an insurmountable barrier. However, the B-2As' work carried on.

During that night, one Spirit crewman noted his solitary feelings of flying over the theatre of operations without as much as a single friendly aircraft for company. The B-2s' combined precision and all-weather targeting functions meant that the aircraft were not hindered by nature. Add to this the high reliability of the jet, and one begins to see the vital role that the Spirit played in the operations in the Balkans. B-2A sorties were written into 34 of 53 Air Tasking Orders, for OAF, and only a single sortie was cancelled because of mechanical problems.

On 21 May, the 509th BW flew its last mission in support of OAF. The final tally for the aircraft was more than 45 missions flown, all using Block 30-configured B-2s. During these sorties, the aircraft dropped 1.3 million pounds of ordnance, which worked out to be 11 percent of the total bombs expended. However, the Spirit force had flown less than one percent of the total sorties flown by all jets participating in the conflict.

The statistics get even more impressive, as 90 percent of B-2A GAMs fell within 40 ft of their targets, while the other ten percent still fell within close proximity of their aim points. The net effect of this gave the aircraft an 87 percent destruction rate. As well as dropping the GAMs, the aircraft also expended four 2000-lb GBU-37 anti-bunker weapons. A total of 51 B-2A pilots flew at least a single combat mission, some flew two and a small number flew three.

For Lt Col Bussiere, OAF illustrated the robustness of the 509th team;

'It's a great feeling to be able to serve your nation, and everyone here at Whiteman understood that their efforts had a direct impact on the lethality of the B-2 weapons system – from the cop to the cook, to the guy on the ramp with a wrench. The steely-eyed pilot here that made it across the line and did the nation's work? Well he wouldn't have reached his target without all the other folks around here. One person stumbles and it affects the whole mission.'

There were several lessons which came out of the Balkans campaign, and the B-2A's participation in it. When speaking before the Military Procurement Subcommittee of the Committee on the Armed Services,

House of Representatives, on the bomber's performance during the campaig,. Brig Gen Leroy Barnidge, Commander of the 509th BW during the campaign, was candid about where the aircraft's capabilities needed to be improved. One of the major issues he raised was sortie generation and mission availability. 'It seems to me that we have to do something to increase the per-aircraft sortie rate to something better than one every three to four days'.

The mission readiness rate was a serious issue, given that just six jets were available for operations against Serbia at any one time – the 509th BW had only received nine B-2s at that point. Of the three listed as unavailable, one was in deep maintenance, the second was in the final stages of the Block 30 upgrade and the third was being used for training.

Furthermore, Brig Gen Barnidge also noted that aircrew needed to be able to change targets should the need arise in flight. Congressman Norman Sisisky agreed, stating that 'aircrews ought to be able to re-programme targets while en route'. The subsequent fitment of Link 16 has gone some way to redressing this OAF deficiency.

Yet there were things that also worked well. The early qualification of GAM on the B-2A gave the bomber an important punch that no other platform was able to bring to the fight. This was not because there were no other aircraft which could deploy GAM, but because the stocks, as we have seen, were decidedly limited. 'Thanks to all of this early testing, the B-2 pilots were fully qualified to use GAM when the Kosovo conflict began. Without this action by Congress, we might not have been as successful in the early days of the air campaign when the B-2A was the only aeroplane that could access the skies over Belgrade, and the only aeroplane that could attack anywhere in bad weather', noted Congressman Norm Dicks.

The after-action assessment of the operations over Serbia also shed some light on the additional support which the Spirits received from other aircraft while conducting their missions. In essence, it seems that there were no 'hard and fast' rules as to whether the aircraft would be sent into the danger zone with or without defence suppression assets. Brig Gen Barnidge noted that, 'Although each aircraft flew individualised routings once in the target area, I think it is important to know that we did take advantage of the other capable assets that were in the theater already, such as the EA-6B Prowlers, which jam enemy radars, and the various fighter CAPs and High Speed Anti-Radiation Missile shooters, which provided assurance against both the air-to-air threat as well as the radar-guided Surface-to-Air Missiles and Anti-Aircraft Anti-Armor Weapon systems, and so forth. This was not a permissive environment. As a result of all of this, our missions were planned very carefully and, I think it is fair to say, well executed'.

When performing the missions, the crews were able to get between two and six hours of rest per sortie according to Brig Gen Barnidge, who described these periods as 'short naps which are intended to refresh you, but not long enough to where you get into a deep sleep, which then requires an extended recovery period to come out of. Because of the importance of fatigue management, I asked every crew after they landed how they felt, and how much sleep they had gotten? They all said that they felt good, and all said that they had managed between two and six hours of sleep, in small increments, of course, and of course only one pilot at a time. Perhaps more significantly, they all asked when could they go again. As a result of all of this, getting pilots to fly these missions was not a problem that I was confronted with'.

The B-2A's usage for the duration of the campaign would contrast markedly with subsequent operations over Afghanistan and Iraq in 2001-03. The Spirit remained committed to OAF to the end for three reasons. Firstly, the aircraft's all-weather characteristics were a vital consideration given the appalling weather that routinely plagued the theatre of operations. Secondly, the jet's unique GAM/JDAM capability. And finally, its LO characteristics in the face of robust air defences, which remained a threat throughout the air campaign.

Lt Gen Marvin R 'Marv' Esmond commented that 'there were still SAM assets that we were aware of, and I will not get too specific because of the nature of their classification. But again, it had to do with the tactic that was pursued by the opposition, which was to husband much of the resource (air defence capability). That lesson is being learned around the world, we believe. The adoption of this tactic is caused by the reputation of US air power. Our enemies know that if they bring it out (aircraft, SAMs and AAA), there is a strong possibility that they will lose it.

'We found that the Serbs were hesitant to take that chance early on, so by the end of OAF there were still some SAM sites that we had to keep an eye on. But in many ways, by virtue of the enemy husbanding those resources, we in effect took them out of play. So while we monitored and watched closely, had the decision been taken to use these weapons, they could have posed a very real threat to us towards the end of the war. We would have undoubtedly been forced to take appropriate action.'

Lt Gen Esmond also noted that the aircraft made a valuable contribution to providing a near-total persistence over the Serbian battlespace. Describing the execution of the OAF air campaign as a tightly choreographed ballet, he said that role of the B-2A 'in the production is to provide that long-range strike capability in all weather, at night, to continue that 24-hour pressure that we needed to put on the Yugoslavian government as part of that ballet, with all the assets with which you are so intimately familiar that bring to bear the total package of air power that kept that pressure on.

'The B-2, because of its reach and its stealthiness could do some things at night that we felt provided the strongest capability to keep that pressure on. We had other platforms available that might perform that role, but again we took advantage of the strength of the B-2 to provide that capability at night where we thought its role ought to be. That was how we integrated it into this particular campaign.'

The B-2A and its GAM payload had a decisive effect on the short but intense final act in the Balkans tragedy. Such was the jet's impact that it was said that Albanian children in refugee camps drew pictures of the bat-winged bomber that had come to defend them and their families. But the final word on how well the B-2A fared in combat, along with its JDAM fist, must go to Ike Skelton, Democratic congressman for Missouri;

'What has happened is that this B-2 stealth bomber from Whiteman, and its (GAM) system, has changed the doctrine of air warfare. This will be a case study for future decades as to how combat in the air proceeds.'

ENDURING FREEDOM

With the Kosovo campaign 'in the bag' as the 509th BW's first combat success, the wing continued to enhance is strengths and its inventory. Its final bomber, *SPIRIT OF AMERICA*, was delivered in Block 30 configuration in early 2000. Block 30 was the most modern incarnation of the aircraft, which featured several new additions to ease the burden of maintenance. Capt David Miller, 325th BS Maintenance Officer, highlighted the jet's improved self-diagnostic capabilities as one of the most important features of the Block 30 B-2s;

'Our mission lives and dies by our ability to quickly and accurately troubleshoot faults. Remarkable improvements in system self-diagnostics empower our technicians to rapidly narrow down the source of the fault, identify corrective measures and return the jet to flying status.'

The number of LO repairs required by Block 30 aircraft in comparison with their predecessors is said to have reduced five-fold. Moreover, the fuselage's aft deck received improvements to 'fine tune' it, as did the rudderons, while the leading edges of the wings were re-engineered.

Almost immediately after the Kosovo campaign had concluded, the B-2A fleet was temporarily grounded and peacetime training missions suspended. The culprit for the suspension was a potential fault discovered in the aircraft's ejection seat initiator, which was then rectified by manufacturer OEA Aerospace. By 8 August 1999, four aircraft were cleared to resume flying operations, with the rest of the fleet following shortly afterwards. 509th BW CO, Brig Gen Barnidge, commented that the grounding 'was a strictly a precautionary measure. There is never a reason to needlessly subject any of our aircrew to increased risk. Suspending our peacetime flying training was a prudent thing to do'.

The hiatus between combat over Serbia and the forthcoming operations over Afghanistan represented useful time during which 509th BW personnel could continue to practise stretching their legs with 'Global Power' missions. In June 2001, 90 members of the wing deployed to Andersen AFB to perform a 12-day 'Global Power' mission under the exercise codename of *Coronet Spider*. The unit supplied to Guam from the 509th was from the 325th BS, redesignated the 325th Expeditionary Bomb Squadron (EBS) for the duration of the deployment.

The intention of the exercise was to practise the forward deployment of the aircraft – something that Whiteman personnel tirelessly practice. The 325th EBS also included members of the 509th Security Forces Squadron, elements of the 393rd BS and also the 50th Operation Support Squadron.

During the exercises, the 325th EBS flew a total of 14 sorties using only three aircraft. In many ways, this operation mirrored those that the 509th

US Defense Secretary Donald H Rumsfeld receives a briefing from 509th BW commanders on how the bomber has been performing against Taleban and al-Qaeda elements in Afghanistan. Deploying the B-2 did generate controversy, with some critics believing that the USAF did not need to send such a high-value asset to the theatre. However, its bomb load, range and discretion were of major importance in the war's early stages (*USAF*)

BW would later perform in the Afghan and Iraq theatres in so much that it would see a small number of bombers performing a relatively large number of sorties. However, unlike the Afghan and Iraq operations, these missions were of around a ten-hour duration, rather than the 30+ hour efforts flown from Whiteman during these campaigns.

A month before getting down to business in OEF, crews from Whiteman had flown an epic 50-hour mission in the B-2A WST on base. All aspects of the sortie were mirrored as accurately as possible. Pilots had to respond to accurately-depicted 'real-world' threats and targets. The scenario had them flying from Whiteman, refuelling six times, striking targets and then landing at an overseas base. It could have almost been one of the missions that the 393rd BS would later fly over Afghanistan.

Once the simulation got underway, crews were not permitted to leave the simulator. Everything that they would need was taken with them into the WST, including sleeping bags, food, water, helmets and ejection seat harnesses. The trusty foldable cot also went.

As with the Kosovo campaign, the personnel at Whiteman had scant warning as to exactly when they would be participating in the Global War On Terror (GWOT). The attacks on New York City and Washington DC on 11 September 2001 literally came out of the blue, but there was little doubt that US retaliation would follow, and that al-Qaeda, accused of masterminding the atrocities, and its Taleban militia cohorts would be the targets.

Less than a month after the attacks, the US military was ready to take the war to the extremists. For the 509th BW, however, the beginning of the conflict seemed almost to be a re-run of OAF two years previously. There was little doubt amongst the men and women at Whiteman that they would be getting involved – it was simply a question of when. However, when the call came, the aircrew and personnel had little time to ready themselves for battle. Sgt Beau Turner remembers that 'In OEF we literally had a couple of hours' notice. We went home for the night, and all of a sudden we got the word to come back in and we took off (for Diego Garcia). We knew what we were going to do, and we were pretty psyched up about it'.

On 5 October 2001 a single B-2A from the 393rd BS made the 509th BW's first strike of the war when it dropped a GBU-37/B 'Bunker Buster' bomb on a suspected al-Qaeda installation in Afghanistan. The jet had flown all of the way from Whiteman AFB to its target, the details of which still remain highly classified.

B-2As (sometimes in pairs) participated in the first three days of OEF, hitting targets all over Afghanistan from Whiteman and then flying on to Diego Garcia, in the Indian Ocean. By the third day of the conflict, all six aircraft which had participated in the action had returned home. It is thought that neither the Taleban nor al-Qaeda made any attempt to engage the jets, not that they would have had the air defences to have even attempted such an act. One spokesman from Whiteman noted that 'as far as we know, they didn't even see us'.

Maj Gen Anthony F Przybyslawski, who was commanding the 509th BW at the time, commented on what the B-2A brought to the fight. 'Four simple words describe our mission – global strike, precision engagement'. The importance of the attacks was keenly felt by all of those at Whiteman who were involved with them. As generations of groundcrews and armourers had done before them, messages were chalked onto the munitions, 'NYPD' (New York Police Department) and 'FDNY' (Fire Department of New York) being amongst the most popular.

Sgt Kelly Costa says that the feelings prior to the OEF missions at Whiteman were palpable;

'I've been working in maintenance my whole life, and I was lucky enough to launch that first aircraft on the B-2's debut combat mission in OAF back in 1999. That was exciting, as I had grown up working on B-52s standing nuclear alert, and I used to spend day after day working on bombers that never got to perform their mission because that was how the Cold War was fought. I never got to go anywhere with the B-52, or launch one on a combat sortie. Then I came to the B-2, and I actually thought it was going to be a long time before we got to participate in OEF, because it seemed like they weren't going to call us into combat for a while.

'It was fantastic to be able to launch that aircraft for *Enduring Freedom* from here, and then deploy to the FOL and watch our aeroplane taxiing out with maybe eight or ten B-52s behind it. I actually got briefed by the pilots before they were taking off, and they explained to me where they were going. We got their aeroplane ready, loading everything aboard that they needed so that they could safely conduct this exhausting mission. The excitement and the thrill of talking to them, and seeing exactly where they were going, and to see the jet break ground and do the mission for real as a team was a fantastic thing.'

The B-2A flights from Whiteman lasted around 40 hours after take-off. The aircraft were refuelled six times during the missions, and once the jets had dropped their bombs they flew on to Diego Garcia. Having landed at the latter base, the aircraft was refuelled and a replacement crew then flew it on a 30-hour mission back to Whiteman.

Amazingly, in the wake of the first mission on 5 October, the aircraft returned home with no requirement for extra maintenance. This effectively meant that the B-2 was ready to perform the same mission all over again. Maj Gen Przybyslawski noted that 'the fact that these aircraft never shut down their engines for more than 70 hours highlights the durability and reliability of the weapons system'. This particular sortie currently holds the record for the longest bombing mission ever flown.

Despite the length of the OEF sorties, Lt Col Steve Basham remembers that staying alert was not necessarily a problem;

'There is no concern with an individual staying awake. When you're going into combat, the sheer adrenaline will carry you all the way through the flight. Then there is an enormous let down as soon as you come out, and now

you've still got to get back home when you're on the other side of the world. That's really the place where we utilise the techniques that are designed to keep us going. You're always busy in the cockpit. There's several things that you need to do throughout the flight, and you can work through those mental challenges.'

The lessons which had been learnt from the days of flying sorties to Yugoslavia were reapplied once again for the missions to Afghanistan. The foldable cot, which was arguably the most inexpensive piece of B-2A equipment ever procured, was utilised to allow the crews to get some rest. Some reports also talked about the pilots completing crosswords, reading or discussing sports on the long flights to and from the combat area.

Lt Col Thomas Bussiere similarly notes that both the crews and the aircraft were well prepared for such long duration missions;

'The bread and butter of the B-2 is to be able to take off from CONUS and go anywhere in the world and make an impact. So we centre all of our training, all of our focus on the ability to do that, and we regularly practise long-duration missions that last for more than 24 hours. We practise long-duration "sims", and we basically have a long-duration check-out programme

An MHU-83C/E munitions loading truck uplifts the B-2A's 'tools of the trade' in OEF, namely a 2000-lb GPS-guided bomb, which is being retrieved from a MHU-110 Munitions Handling Trailer
(*TSgt Janice H Cannon*)

Lights blazing in the rain, a B-2A taxies out of the maintenance hangar at Whiteman in preparation for its first ever mission in support of OEF. During the opening stages of the conflict, the combination of B-2As and ship-launched Tomahawk Land Attack Missiles were imperative in taking the war back to the aggressors with a series of clinical strikes
(*SSgt Michael Gaddis*)

for our pilots, where we train them to deal with both the physical and physiological aspects of a long duration flight.

'What makes the B-2 unique is that there are only two aviators in the aircraft. We don't have spare pilots or spare crew members who can swap in on a 36-hour mission. It is critical to manage who is sleeping when, and to make sure that those rest periods work in well with the mission-critical events in flight, whether that be air-refuelling or weapons employment over the target area.'

Interestingly, the thought of being the first in and the first out does not always lead to increased stress for the pilots;

'The B-2 is generally the first one to kick down the door, but that does not necessarily lead to an increased stress level. It's actually a matter of pride for the community, as really that's our bread and butter – it's what we do, and it's all part of building the B-2 combat aviator.'

Col Eric Single echoes the importance of the B-2A in breaking a hole in the enemy's defences;

'Obviously as a Global Bomber, what we bring to the fight is similar to other bombers. We have the range, we have the payload and we have the precision weapons capability that is in pretty high demand for this type of asset. What we bring to the fight that the other bombers don't have is the low observability, or the stealthiness, of the jet. We can be used in that role, as we have the capability to target the command and control assets that are the eyes and ears of the enemy. The jet's stealthiness basically means that the B-2 shrinks the ranges at which an enemy radar can see it, creating holes in the integrated air defence network which can be exploited to allow the bomber to get in closer to the target.'

The use of the aircraft in OEF did generate some controversy, however. To paraphrase US Defense Secretary Donald H Rumsfeld's comment about President Bill Clinton's decision to perform cruise missile attacks on Afghan al-Qaeda targets in 1998 in retaliation for the attacks on the US embassies in Dar-es-Salaam, Tanzania, and Nairobi, Kenya, 'What is the point of sending a one million dollar missile to hit a ten dollar tent?'

Well, the answer seems fairly straightforward. Yes, there were aircraft in the USAF inventory which could have performed a similar attack on 5 October 2001 – the B-52H and B-1B both have impressive weapons payloads, and both have the range and experience to perform ultra-long range attacks. However, both have relatively large crews – five for the B-52H and four for the B-1B. Why place more crewmembers at risk over an extremely hostile environment than you have to? With a Spirit, only two members are at risk.

Secondly, both the Stratofortress and the Lancer would require a strike package of aircraft to perform fighter escort and defence suppression. Yes, the air defences of Afghanistan were almost prehistoric, but no military planner in their right mind would take the risk. Secondly, the strike package places more crews at risk. The B-2A has its defensive systems built in via its' LO characteristics and defensive electronics, thus obviating the need for the escorts.

There is another argument in the the B-2A's favour – it has a unique capability, being able to carry all-important 'bunker-busting' weapons. US Intelligence knew that al-Qaeda leader Osama bin Laden had chosen to place key elements of his organisations' infrastructure deep within the rugged mountain landscape of Afghanistan, as the battles in the Tora Bora cave complex in southeastern Afghanistan would later show.

The B-2A, placing fewer aircrew at risk, with its LO characteristics and its 'bunker busting' ordnance made it an ideal choice for the first few days of OEF. One political pundit commented that the use of the aircraft was 'simply a demonstration of unique American technological capabilities. It's essentially unrelated to the actual operational requirements. We spent $40 billion on them, so we better use them for something. If they want to get into the fight and do their part for the war effort, I'm not going to complain'.

While the bomber is indeed a unique demonstration of American technological capabilities, it is difficult to imagine any USAF general deciding to place an aircraft as valuable and expensive as the B-2A into combat if the circumstances did not require him to. Maj Gen Henry Osmon, a senior officer at the Pentagon's Joint Staff, told a press conference at the time of the operation that the decision as to whether the Spirit would be used or not 'really belongs to the regional commander overseeing the war – in this case Army Gen Tommy Franks – and depends on the target he wants to strike and the munitions needed to hit them on a particular day'.

However, the waters were muddied further when an unnamed Pentagon official was asked why the Spirits were used when carrier-based aircraft were closer to the theatre of operations. He replied 'because we can. There's no good reason'. One good reason, however, might have been that despite the US Navy having carriers located closer to Afghanistan in the Arabian Gulf, naval aviators would still have to face flights lasting up to eight hours in aircraft that could not carry the all important anti-bunker weapons of the B-2A. Spirit crews had already

JDAM are loaded into one of the Spirit's two bomb-bays as the aircraft is prepared for the opening phases of the GWOT. Such operations with 2000-lb bombs require a well-balanced mix of strength and delicacy on the part of the armourers involved (*MSgt Michael R Nixon*)

SPIRIT OF AMERICA undergoes a maintenance check, having participated in OEF. The forms held in the airman's hands contain details of the systems and airframe components which must be checked upon the aircraft's return from a mission (*MSgt Michael R Nixon*)

perfected the art of performing extraordinarily long missions from Whiteman during OAF. Finally, Navy aircraft would still require a supporting strike package, thus increasing the number of crews sent into the unknown.

The final word on the debate should go to Lt Col Bussiere, who argues that using the B-2A brought a simple advantage to the United States;

'When America goes to war, generally we like to have the upper hand and hit with the force of power required to kick down the door. During the first couple of days of *Enduring Freedom*, although our intelligence community had great assay on the threats out there, we wanted to make sure that the deck was stacked and we could lay the conditions for follow-on forces. I can see how people can look at OAF and OEF and say that the threat levels were different, and indeed they were. But the capabilities and the impact that the B-2 made on the first few nights of both conflicts, and any future wars for that matter, outweighed any concern that the threat level may have been too low for the B-2'.

Lt Col Basham agreed;

'The aircraft, without a doubt, has spoken for itself. It has also spoken for the entire Whiteman AFB team, the entire Air Force team and our entire military. We go in, and just as in *Allied Force*, *Enduring Freedom* and *Iraqi Freedom*, we don't do anything in half measures – you just can't take any chances. I'd much rather say we over-prepared than to come back on the other side and say we made a mistake because we weren't prepared.

'Not only did the taxpayers get what they paid for in the interim with the B-2, this aircraft, because of its capability and because of its unique characteristics and things coming on line, continues to grow as a viable asset. So whereas maybe other assets in the past have had a very limited life, the Spirit is actually going very much further into the future, and it is adapting as our enemies adapt to this aircraft. It has proven itself, and now it's well-poised for the future.'

CONCLUSIONS

'Certainly in Afghanistan, the degree of accuracy and the amount of weaponry that the aircraft could deliver on target, and the fact that it could deliver to multiple targets on the same mission, were all things which enhanced its capabilities in OEF', remembers James Kinnu.

All of the Spirits dropped their munitions from high altitude, thought to be around 50,000 ft. This displays the degree of trust which USAF planners had in the accuracy of their munitions. The first three days of the conflict saw a total of six B-2A missions. This averaged around two missions per day, although it is thought that only a single aircraft flew on the first night of the war.

During the six OEF combat missions which the aircraft performed in the first few days of the war, B-2s hit the following targets – air defence and airfield sites in Shebergan, Mazar-e-Sharif and Kunduz, along with an enemy troop garrison also in northern Afghanistan. Other targets included command and control, airfield, air defence, garrison and terrorist targets near the capital Kabul and Jalalabad, in the eastern part of the country. Terrorist and air defence targets were struck in southern Afghanistan near Kandahar and Moqor, while still more air defence sites and airfields were bombed in the western part of the country near Shindand and Herat. One of these attacks saw a direct hit achieved on an airfield's runway.

The profile for the missions was to take off from Whiteman and fly directly towards the targets in Afghanistan. Having performed their attacks, the aircraft would then head for Diego Garcia to refuel and change crew. The replacement crew would fly the aircraft directly back to the United States.

OEF's high mission tempo had an adverse effect on the mission-capable rates of the aircraft as the campaign progressed. At the start of the war, the aircraft had a 55 percent mission-capable rate – i.e. around nine aircraft were available at any one point for missions. However, by November, by which time B-2A sorties over Afghanistan had concluded, the mission-capable rate had dropped to just eight jets available.

Throughout 2001, the air force had been under pressure to increase the mission availability of the aircraft. The goal had been set that year for a mission-capable rate of 60 percent (ten aircraft), but the average rate for the year was just 31 percent (five aircraft) – some 50 percent below the USAF's expectations. The previous year, the mission-capable rate had been 37 percent (six aircraft).

Why was this gap in expectations emerging? Quite simply because of the aircraft's low-observibality maintenance requirements. Repairs to the aircraft's skin are time-consuming to say the least. The materials required to keep the stealth bomber obscured on radars are delicate, highly specialised and take time to apply and to cure. So awkward are these procedures that if the aircraft had not required such delicate treatment, then it was anticipated that the mission-capable rate would have been around 80 percent (14 aircraft).

A wing check is performed on a B-2A after its arrival back at Whiteman. As in every conflict in which it has participated, Spirits were thoroughly inspected both inside and out before and after a mission. Despite this, the sortie readiness rate for the B-2A fell below expectations at certain times during OEF (*SSgt Shane Cuomo*)

Two members of the 509th's Maintenance Squadron perform a finger-tip inspection of this Spirit's fuselage. Such work is carried out to ensure that the aircraft has not sustained any damage to its all important stealth skin. The airmen wear safety wires to cushion their fall should they slip off the smooth fuselage (*MSgt Michael R Nixon*)

A B-2A taxies in to the Andersen AFB base FOL soon after the 509th BW's commitment to OEF had come to an end (*USAF*)

One report argued that other problems afflicting the 509th BW included a shortage of fully-qualified LO maintainers. There was also an accusation that senior officers in the wing had elected to ensure that the aircraft met its flying hour programme, and to this end deferred LO maintenance. Interestingly, if the LO repairs were not included when evaluating the mission-capable rate, then the availability of the aircraft would have been around 80 percent (14 aircraft). Other maintenance issues included the time taken for post-flight and operations inspections, the failure of power take-off shafts, phase inspections for the jet and the failure of engine inlet seals.

The Air Force has tried hard to improve the aircraft's capabilities in combat, and to this end it continues to run a test and evaluation programme with the 72nd Test and Evaluation Squadron (TES) at Edwards AFB, California. In 2001, shortly before the commencement of OEF, the 72nd TES used its B-2A to evaluate the performance of the aircraft against undisclosed threat systems – presumably new surface-to-air missiles, radar systems and air-to-air weapons. This work is vital if the aircraft is to stay fully abreast of current and anticipated future threats. Failure to do this would place the B-2 at a major disadvantage, endangering the lives of the crew.

To ensure that the aircraft can operate with maximum flexibility, the Air Force has also invested in the procurement of deployable shelters for the B-2 which have been constructed at bases on the islands of Diego Garcia and Guam. Shelters have also been designated for erection at RAF Fairford. Prior to the deployment of these semi-permanent, climate-controlled structures in which the B-2As LO materials can be maintained and repaired, a test of the B-2 Shelter System (B2SS) was conducted at Whiteman in June 2001. The assembly and dismantling of a B2SS was performed three times, with each assembly taking around 30 days. The trials also illustrated that the structures require concrete pads and utilities to operate properly.

Because of these findings, the USAF decided to maintain the B2SS installations as semi-permanent facilities at its FOLs. Just as the 9/11 attacks occurred, a decision was made to procure four shelter systems and to upgrade the prototype B2SS at Whiteman to a production-level configuration. By April 2002, the first systems were prepared for deployment, with the initial system being made 'deployment ready'.

COLOUR PLATES

1
B-2A 93-1087 *SPIRIT OF PENNSYLVANIA*,
393rd BS/509th BW, Whiteman AFB,
September 1997

2
B-2A 93-1086 *SPIRIT OF KITTY HAWK*,
13th BS/509th BW, Whiteman AFB,
October 2005

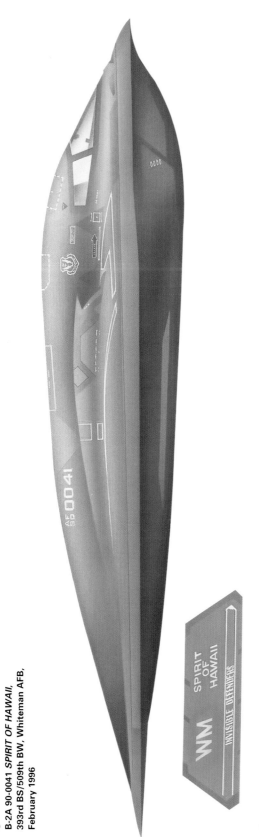

3
B-2A 90-0041 SPIRIT OF HAWAII,
393rd BS/509th BW, Whiteman AFB,
February 1996

4
B-2A 88-0329 SPIRIT OF MISSOURI,
13th BS/509th BW, Whiteman AFB,
September 2005

5
B-2A 82-1071 *SPIRIT OF MISSISSIPPI*,
325th BS/509th BW, Whiteman AFB,
October 2001

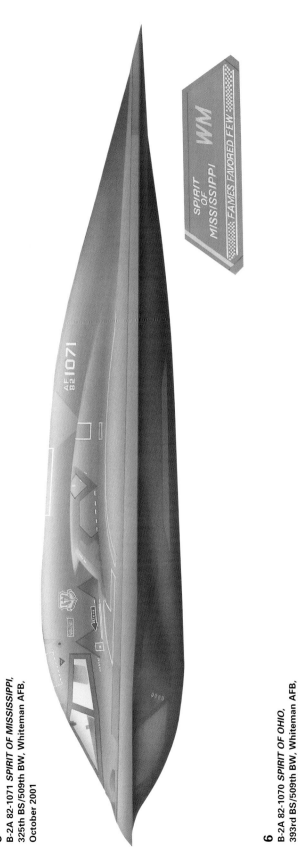

6
B-2A 82-1070 *SPIRIT OF OHIO*,
393rd BS/509th BW, Whiteman AFB,
January 1997

7
B-2A 89-0127 *SPIRIT OF KANSAS*,
393rd BS/509th BW, Whiteman AFB,
July 1997

8
B-2A 93-1085 *SPIRIT OF OKLAHOMA*,
393rd BS/509th BW, Whiteman AFB,
December 1998

9
B-2A 82-1066 *SPIRIT OF AMERICA*,
393rd BS/509th BW, Whiteman AFB,
October 2001

10
B-2A 82-1068 *SPIRIT OF NEW YORK*,
410th TS/412th TW, Edwards AFB,
January 1996

11
B-2A 89-0128 *SPIRIT OF NEBRASKA*,
393rd BS/509th BW, Whiteman AFB,
September 1995

12
B-2A 90-0040 *SPIRIT OF ALASKA*,
393rd BS/509th BW, Whiteman AFB,
March 1996

13
B-2A 88-0328 *SPIRIT OF TEXAS,*
393rd BS/509th BW, Whiteman AFB,
February 1996

14
B-2A 88-0332 *SPIRIT OF WASHINGTON,*
325th BS/509th BW, Whiteman AFB,
June 1995

15
B-2A 88-0330 *SPIRIT OF CALIFORNIA*,
13th BS/509th BW, Whiteman AFB,
December 2005

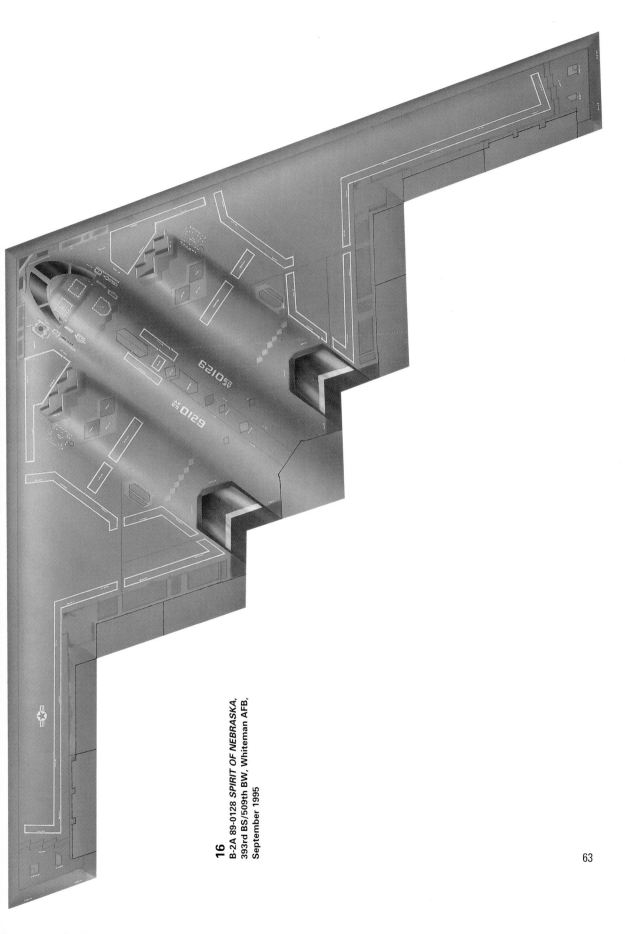

16
B-2A 89-0128 *SPIRIT OF NEBRASKA*,
393rd BS/509th BW, Whiteman AFB,
September 1995

63

IRAQI FREEDOM

To date, the B-2A had seen action in two different theatres. Serbia had been festooned with a highly integrated air defence system, albeit seemingly switched off for most of the time. Afghanistan's air defence system, on the other hand, did not seem to extend beyond a few shoulder-launched Stinger missiles and a selection of ZSU-23-4 multi-barrelled anti-aircraft guns. The third test for the Spirit would almost immediately follow its engagement in Afghanistan, and like Serbia, the adversary would have a potent air defence capability.

US and British aircraft had been wearing down Iraq's air defences for almost 15 years since the imposition of the Northern and Southern no-fly zones following the end of the first Gulf War in 1991. Yet Saddam had refused to bow to international pressure, and he had been suspected of enhancing his air defences through clandestine purchases of foreign technology and equipment to make those systems which he did still possess thoroughly connected and robust in the event of another onslaught

A B-2A unsticks from the main runway at Diego Garcia on its way to strike targets in Iraq during a typically tropical day in late March 2003 (*TSgt Janice H Cannon*)

While Saddam's air defences might have seen better days, the USAF was not going to risk non-stealthy aircraft over the 'SuperMEZ' unless it absolutely had to. To this end, the B-2A became an essential part of the initial war effort, until such defences were suitably worn down for their non-stealth brethren (*USAF*)

by the United States and its allies. James Kinnu noted that 'certainly, in the early days of Operation *Iraqi Freedom*, Iraqi air defences were reasonably good, but the Spirits were able to operate unscathed, undetected and were able to destroy all of the infrastructure. It speaks highly for the aeroplane'.

OUTFOXED

The B-2A had not yet seen combat in the skies of the Middle East. It had missed out on Operation *Desert Storm* as it was not yet in service, and it had sat out Operation *Desert Fox* seven years later. The latter was a high-tempo series of intense air strikes which occurred against Saddam over a 96-hour period in December 1998 as retaliation for his expulsion of United Nations weapons inspectors from Iraq. At the time, the B-2 stayed on the ramp to ensure that the nuclear deterrent remained sharp while its USAF brethren went to work on Iraq's military infrastructure.

This is not to say that the B-2A was considered irrelevant to this theatre. The aircraft almost had its Arabian debut in Operation *Desert Thunder* in early 1998. This operation, which would later metamorphose into *Desert Fox*, was prepared in retaliation for Saddam's obstruction of UN weapons inspectors as they sought to investigate his suspected Weapons of Mass Destruction (WMD) facilities, particularly his so-called 'Presidential Palaces'. In the true tradition of the Iraqi leader, he backed down at the last minute from a showdown with the United States and the United Kingdom.

As the date for *Desert Thunder* drew closer, the 509thBW was alerted and told to ready an undisclosed number of jets to join the action. Yet Saddam's climb-down ensured that the B-2s stayed on the ramp for now, and *Desert Thunder* instead became the codename for the build-up of Coalition aircraft in the region prior to *Desert Fox*. Saddam's cooperation with the international community did not last long, however, and he resumed his political chicanery with the weapons inspectors and began to violate the no-fly zone. Indeed, on one occasion he even threatened to down a USAF U-2 reconnaissance aircraft.

The stage was set for Operation *Desert Fox*, during which the B-2's B-1B cousins took the war to the Iraqi despot on 16 December 1998. After having been placed on alert to perform in this action, the Spirit once again took a back seat, and the combat action lasted only four days.

'GLOBAL POWER'

The time in between OEF and OIF did not see the 509th BW simply remaining stationary and waiting for action. Despite the waging of the GWOT, the B-2As and their personnel continued to train as they fight, and to continually practise the global deployments which are such a vital part of their mission and their effect.

In December 2002, three B-2As made a voyage to Hickam AFB in Hawaii. The deployment was part of an initiative to train members of the 25th Air Support Operations Squadron (ASOS). During their stay on the island, the aircraft dropped Mk 82 practice bombs (the inert version of the Mk 84) on the Pohakuloa Training Area. This was the first time that the B-2A community had been able to train in Hawaii. For the 25th ASOS, the visit was also significant given that the unit is more used to training with F-15, F-16 and F/A-18 aircraft, along with the B-1B and the B-52H. Capt Todd Moore, air liaison officer with the 25th ASOS, told the press that the

A B-2A sits alongside a B-52H at Diego Garcia in March 2003. Both aircraft have played a vital role in the GWOT in both major theatres. Ground and flightcrews mingle in front of the aircraft (*TSgt Richard Freeland*)

An indication of just how much US air power was ranged against Iraq from Diego Garcia in OIF is clearly visible in this view of a crowded ramp in late March 2003 (*TSgt Richard Freeland*)

visit had been a long time in the making. 'Usually, the B-2 is reserved for combat only. We've been working on this visit for more than a year'.

The Spirit's debut in Hawaiian skies clearly had a marked effect on the local population. Local resident Henry Williams was moved to remark that 'at 5.30 pm, Hawaii Standard Time, 11 December, my wife and I saw one of the most beautiful sights I can remember. Two B-2s made three passes over our coffee farm on the Big Island. They were flying into a gorgeous tropical sunset that is common this time of the year. I want to tell you that our "patriotic thermometer" went off the scale. It made us proud to be Americans, and free. To be citizens of a country that could produce such a magnificent machine is truly an honour.

'Let us not forget that those two aircraft were crewed by our country's finest and best-trained people. They are out doing their jobs so that we can enjoy our liberties and our lives. Ever aware of the mission that the B-2 is designed for, we hope that they will be safe and secure.'

A wise message, given that the B-2A would be entering combat shortly against the very regime that it almost attacked in 1998. Given the acute secrecy of the Spirit's participation in the conflict, the 509th BW was very quiet on whether it would be participating in any military action. This seemed almost certain, however, given that the war clouds over Iraq were already gathering by the end of 2002 amid political manoeuvrings at the UN and strident spin emanating from Washington and London about taking the Iraqi leader to task.

Col Doug Raaberg, CO of the 509th BW, laconically noted that his aircraft and personnel would be ready 'in case we get the call'. Speculation in the media and by defence pundits across the world was that the B-2A would be joining in the action – they would not be disappointed.

Confirmation arrived on 30 October 2002 when Col Raaberg announced that the 509th BW would be forward-deployed to the island of Diego Garcia, in the Indian Ocean. At the time, the unit was performing exercises at RAF Fairford.

Despite the B-2A having flown to Diego Garcia after the strikes on Afghanistan, the deployment of the jet to the Indian Ocean would mark the first occasion that it had been sent to a FOL for wartime operations.

The US government had already asked its British counterpart for permission to build the special climatically-controlled hangers on the island in preparation for the deployment. Given that Diego Garcia is still technically a British protectorate, with basing facilities leased to the US armed forces, requests such as these have to be sent to London. A Royal Navy officer remains in charge of the facility, and any request to use it for military operations must first be cleared by the Prime Minister. However, given the support that the UK government was offering to the Bush administration *vis-à-vis* Saddam's removal, it is difficult to image such a request being refused.

Shortly before OIF kicked off, the *Financial Times* in London published a satellite photograph of Diego Garcia, which showed two of the hangers constructed and ready to receive their occupants. At this point, however, there still did not appear to be any of the 509th BW's assets on the ramp.

Following the construction of the shelters, the stage was set for a deployment to this 'unsinkable aircraft carrier' off the coast of East Africa. A redeployment of B-1Bs, which were already based at Diego Garcia, to Thumrait, Oman, gave additional ramp space for the B-2As. Effectively, the USAF was now giving the message that any action against Iraq would see the US spearheading the air campaign with the Spirits. Moreover, it was sending a message to Saddam that the US and its allies were perfectly serious about military action and regime change.

During Operation *Desert Storm*, it was the F-117A Nighthawk that had been so important in punching a hole through the air defences which the Iraqi leader had purchased to safeguard his domain. Moreover, these defences were integrated via sophisticated fibre-optic networks, had been constructed in a layered fashion and were centrally controlled. The Nighthawk was the only aircraft which was up to the job in 1991, and by destroying key air defence command and control nodes, this opened the way for follow-on non-LO aircraft to enter Iraqi airspace and hit various targets. It was clear that on this occasion the B-2A would be doing a similar job, albeit with more weapons than the two-munition payload of the F-117A.

The opening phase of the attack was dubbed 'Shock and Awe' by Pentagon spin-doctors, and it was designed to deliver a spectacular blow to Saddam's security and military apparatus. The plan was two fold – first of all, to destroy as much of the command and control of the Iraqi armed forces as possible in order to ease the workload of follow-on air and ground forces, and to leave the Iraqi military punch-drunk and demoralised. Secondly, it was hoped that such a display of power and determination by the US-led Coalition would persuade the Iraqi government that resistance was futile, and that the best course of action would be Saddam's resignation.

There was just one problem. The Iraqi capital Baghdad was ring-fenced by a thick curtain of surface-to-air missiles and anti-aircraft artillery known as the 'SuperMEZ' (Super Missile Engagement Zone). The only way of getting through this unscathed and destroying the targets would be to use stand-off sea- and air-launched cruise missiles and stealthy aircraft such as the F-117A and the B-2A. The B-1B, which is also suitably small

MSgt Kelly Costa performs the final checks on the *SPIRIT OF MISSISSIPPI* before it enters combat over Iraq. The opening phases of OIF were said to have witnessed the largest insertion of USAF bombers since the Vietnam War (*TSgt Janice H Cannon*)

in appearance on radar, would also join the attack. Lt Matthew Hasson from the 509th BW summed up his colleagues' role. 'Our primary job is kicking the door down. We clear out the integrated air defences that pose a direct threat to the other, less-stealthy airframes'. The Spirits would also go after military communications sites and leadership targets.

GIMME SHELTER

Prior to the commencement of hostilities, the 509th BW moved four B-2As to Diego Garcia in preparation for their attacks. Sgt Beau Turner recalled how important the new shelters were to him and his colleagues as they made the aircraft available for sorties;

'We actually saw the shelters at work doing exactly what they were supposed to do. You can't just take materials, glues and paints and apply them in any environment. At times, some of our FOLs are a little bit colder than others, some are a little bit warmer than others and some get very hot inside. Nevertheless, the shelters provided us with an environmentally controlled space to allow us to conduct 24/7 operations.

'We have far more flexibility by being closer to the area of interest, having the ability to turn around aircraft a lot quicker. We also maintain the capability to strike from the CONUS. The latter allows us to launch strikes from Whiteman before anybody knows what's going on, just as we did in OEF and OIF. Before the enemy knows what has happened, the B-2s have already struck the target and are on their way back home.

'By going to the FOL, we were able to turn our jets around a lot faster. Having them forward deployed also sends out a powerful message to potential enemies. Within hours you can have those jets wherever you want them to be, rather than such operations taking days.'

For Sgt Turner, the sight of seeing the B-2As go into battle from Diego Garcia for the first time on 21 March filled him with great pride;

'I can't tell you how proud I felt as the jets left the FOL. Everyone works long shifts, and I think that day when we knew it was kicking off, there wasn't a maintainer on that island not watching the orchestration of bombers departing. To be a bomber guy seeing B-52s taking off laden down with JDAM, followed by our B-2s, was just an awesome feeling. It was US air power at its best – I get goose bumps just thinking about it.'

Everyone in the 509th BW was working extremely hard to get the jets ready for the sorties, and to ensure that the tempo of operations with the B-2A was maintained once OIF began. Sgt Turner remarked that 'Our maintainers work extremely long hours day in, day out. When you have to work all kinds of hours generating sorties, you have to firmly believe in what your doing, and what you're nation's doing. That way the adrenaline stays with you. I don't know if I was tired once. You just forget about minor inconveniences like sleep'.

Normal working hours went out of the window once the operations

Quietly creeping towards its targets, this B-2A was loaded up with munitions that reduced key Iraqi targets to rubble during the 'Shock and Awe' phase of the air campaign (*SSgt Cherie A Thurlby*)

Capt Jennifer Wilson dons her parachute harness in the Life Support shop at Nellis AFB during a *Red Flag* exercise. The parachute harness is but one item of life support equipment which the crews must wear when flying the B-2. Capt Wilson was the first woman to fly a B-2 into combat during OIF (*MSgt Michael R Nixon*)

***SPIRIT OF CALIFORNIA* taxies out for a mission from its Diego Garcia base during the opening strikes of OIF (*SSgt Michael Gaddis*)**

got underway. Sgt Kelly Costa can 'remember being there for 14, 15 or 16 hours. I wasn't supposed to work beyond my 12-hour shift, but you know what, it didn't matter. The main thing was that the job got done, and we got it done right. The pilot depends on everything on that aircraft. It's a team effort because everybody's got a piece in that pie. We have to do our job properly so that the pilot can go and do his. It's a team effort'.

While OIF marked the first occasion that the B-2A had forward deployed for hostile action, it was also the first time that women had flown the aircraft into combat. Capt Jennifer Wilson had arrived at Diego Garcia with the four jets of the 393rd BS (redesignated as the 393rd Expeditionary Bomb Squadron (EBS), part of the 40th Air Expeditionary Wing) for the latter stages of the operation, flying into the base on 1 April. Like all B-2A pilots who would participate in OIF, fear was at the back of her mind. 'Flying is great. I can't imagine doing anything else right now, and to be able to have a chance to fly in combat with the B-2 is an awesome experience'.

Capt Wilson had previously flown B-1Bs, most notably during OAF, so she was not new to combat;

'For me, it's exciting to be a part of a chosen few. I am lucky to be able to have the chance to do something that so few people will ever have the opportunity to do. I wasn't scared. We've all trained quite a bit leading up to this operation. I knew I was going to be able to come through and get the job done. It was just great coming off the aeroplane and seeing the people who came to show me support. From the maintainers to the operators, I was humbled to see them excited for me. We all work together to make the missions happen.'

The Diego Garcia decision was to be instrumental in the war. Up until OIF, the B-2A had always had to perform its missions from Missouri, flying all the way to the combat zone, which necessitated exhaustively long sorties. However, the island base was just a mere five hours away from downtown Baghdad. This proximity translated into less crew fatigue and less wear and tear on the aircraft. Moreover, given that the B-2 was closer to the combat zone, it could generate more sorties and place more pressure on the Iraqi armed forces and government. While only four jets were deployed in OIF, having them five hours away became a serious force multiplier.

Cynics at the time had asked the question about what air defences there actually were in Iraq to attack, given the 15 years of attrition via the enforcement of the no-fly zones? However, Saddam had remained far

The B-2As were able to generate more missions and thus become force multipliers by flying from Diego Garcia during OIF. The aircraft had recovered to this tropical base following OEF strikes in 2001, so the personnel of the 509th had some experience of operating from this remote location (*TSgt Richard Freeland*)

Capt Marty Schulting checks a pre-flight inspection point on a Spirit. Meanwhile, a crew chief briefs him on the status of his aircraft, *SPIRIT OF ALASKA*, prior to its participation in a bombing mission during OIF (*MSgt Michael R Nixon*)

from quiet during the years following *Desert Storm*. Certainly, UN sanctions had gripped Iraq, making the open purchase of military equipment all but impossible. However, it is thought that this did not prevent the Iraqi leader from trying to secure defence equipment purchases on the black market, with technology thought to have arrived from Serbia, China, Russia and France.

Some analysts believed that Saddam had taken advantage of the hiatus in overt military action with the West to covertly improve the air defences which he still possessed with fibre-optic cabling which would improve the connectivity of the radars and the SAM batteries. These communications were also thought to have a degree of redundancy built into them which would enable them to keep functioning even if part of the air defence network was destroyed. The Iraqi president was also thought to have added reinforcement to hardened air defence command and control facilities, to have built new installations and to have added more radars to the network.

Moreover, his air defenders had well over a decade's worth of experience in observing the tactics of US and British warplanes enforcing the no-fly zones, and had taken a leaf out of the Serbian armed force's book, strictly adhering to the rule 'if in doubt, don't switch on your radar'. Yet this policy was a double-edged sword, given that during the decade of UN sanctions enforcing, Coalition pilots had become fully aware of the air defence tactics of their adversaries. Finally, the air defences around Baghdad had never been subjected to the hammering that those in the the no-fly zones had endured, making them something of an unknown quantity.

Prior to the conflict, a report had emerged that the Iraqi government might have procured a radar system from the Czech company Tesla-Par-dubice. This system was possibly capable of providing an actionable

radar picture of both the F-117A and the B-2A. US intelligence officials believed that Iraqi generals had attempted to buy the radar system for $176 million, but that the deal had collapsed after the company went bust.

The Tamara radar system, two of which had been built, had apparently 'disappeared' after the company had folded. One former employee noted that 'Tesla-Pardubice closed in 1998. It had two radar systems that had not been sold, but they have disappeared. Nobody knows where they are'. The Pentagon took the report very seriously, and a spokesman went on the record stating that 'it stands to reason that Iraq would want to get its hands on a radar system capable of detecting stealth bombers. In the Gulf War, it was the early F-117 attacks that put most of their air defences out of commission. But we don't know whether they have such a system at the moment'.

On 27 March 2003 a Spirit would perform one of its most vital missions of the war. US target analysts had identified a command, control and communications centre which was believed to be located within the headquarters of Saddam Hussein's Ba'ath Party in Baghdad. Intelligence reports indicated that this facility was playing a key role in directing guerrilla operations against Coalition troops, and also in organising so-called 'death squads' which were meting out their own brand of summary justice against deserters and those suspected of collaborating with the Coalition.

The facility was earmarked for a B-2A strike. The bomber unleashed a precise and devastating attack on the facility, two EGBU-28 'bunker busting' munitions being delivered with clinical precision. The inside of the building was demolished, sending a massive plume of smoke into the night sky and burying those individuals who had been staffing the bunker. The attack was televised live, and the Pentagon later issued a statement denying that it had used the GBU-43/B Massive Ordnance Air

A B-2A takes on fuel from a KC-135 tanker somewhere over southern Iraq en route to targets once combat had begun. Unlike on previous occasions in this region, there was little doubt that the bomber would be bringing some important 'punch' to the campaign in OIF. The proximity of the B-2As to Iraq during their deployment from Diego Garcia did go some way to helping the 509th BW generate more sorties and reduce aircraft and crew wear and tear. However, the aircraft still required regular aerial refuelling, particularly if they were planning to stay over the combat area for some time (*TSgt Richard Freeland*)

Burst, the biggest non-nuclear munition in the USAF arsenal. The EGBU-28 was the ideal weapon for such an attack, being able to burrow through 29 ft of concrete or 100 ft of soil and dirt, before its 630-lb (285.7-kg) warhead detonated.

The B-2As generated an impressive mission-capable rate of 85 percent during the conflict – a vast improvement on the figures for OEF. During their operations, the stealth bombers were not confined to attacking air defence and high-value hardened targets. On one occasion, a B-2A was said to have received imagery intelligence from an RQ-4A Global Hawk unmanned aerial vehicle, which redirected it to attack elements of the Iraqi Republican Guard 'Medina' Division. The crew were required to re-programme their JDAM weapons en route. On another occasion, a B-2 delivered 80 500-lb Mk 82 'iron' bombs during a single run.

According to the 509th BW, the aircraft was able to fly simultaneous operations from Whiteman and Diego Garcia in OIF. During the conflict, the B-2 flew 43 sorties, striking regime targets, command and control facilities, airfields and fielded forces. One of the most interesting features of the campaign was that the aircraft 'Demonstrated time-sensitive targeting/retargeting operations'.

The B-2 force flew 27 of its 43 sorties from Whiteman for a total of 975.8 hours – an average of around 36 hours per mission. The aircraft

Below left
The aircraft shelters at Whiteman are specially designed with front and rear opening doors which allow the Spirit to start its engines prior to taxiing to the runway. This is an important modification to the hangars, as it allows the aircraft to get airborne as soon as possible once they have taxied out onto the ramp (*TSgt Michael R Nixon*)

Below
AFC Sean Landau is given a weather update from SSgt Brian Gibson prior to a bombing mission from Diego Garcia. The aircraft about to perform the sortie is *SPIRIT OF OKLAHOMA* (*SSgt Michael Gaddis*)

93-1086 *SPIRIT OF KITTY HAWK* is greeted by its groundcrew at Whiteman, having just completed the return flight from Diego Garcia during OIF. The aircraft was deployed with the 325th BS (*USAF*)

SPIRIT OF ARIZONA arrives back at Whiteman having completed its involvement in OIF. While the aircraft were deployed at Diego Garcia, once their participation in the campaign was complete they would recover back to their home base (*MSgt Michael R Nixon*)

dropped a total of 418 munitions. This included 230 GBU-31(V)1 JDAM (the vast majority of the total load), along with 97 GBU-31(V)3 weapons. A total of 11 GBU-37 weapons were dropped by aircraft from Whiteman, while a total of 80 Mk 82s were also deployed, presumably against battlefield targets. Some 20 sorties were also flown from Diego Garcia. The cumulative total number of hours that these missions took was 270.5, with each sortie taking an average of 16.9 hours. During operations from Diego Garcia, the aircraft dropped 217 GBU-31(V)1s, 39 GBU-31(V)3s and two GBU-37s.

TESTING TIMES

OIF I was all but over by mid April, and the B-2s had departed Diego Garcia by 1 May. With their participation in the conflict at an end, it was time to return to Whiteman and resume the familiar routine of upgrades, maintenance, evaluation and training. Part of this effort is conducted by the 412th Test Wing (TW) at Edwards AFB, California, the unit operating the only B-2A not based at Whiteman. Testing and evaluation of the aircraft is very much ongoing, and the jet is regularly qualified for new weapons systems thanks to the activities of the 412th.

In August 2003, the wing conducted tests of the GBU-28B/B GPS/INS guided weapon. A huge 5000-lb device, this bomb is intended to smash the deeply buried targets which the DoD fear could be used to house WMD facilities or command centres in 'countries of concern'. Two such weapons were dropped on 14 August at the Utah Testing and Training Range at Hill AFB, this sortie representing the last flight for the developmental test and evaluation phase of the GBU-28B/B programme.

The GBU-28B/B is an enhanced version of the USAF's GBU-28A/B, which has been specifically designed to operate with the B-2A. The weapon can be guided by either GPS or a laser-guidance system, and is deployable in all weather conditions. Testing of the weapon had originally begun in March 2003, just as the 393rd BW was preparing for its missions over Iraq, when an inert GBU-28B/B was dropped at the China Lake Naval Air Warfare Centre in California. The programme then entered further testing, which was also performed at Hill AFB, during which an inert weapon, this time fitted with a guidance system, was released.

SPIRIT OF MISSOURI comes to rest at Whiteman, having completed its deployment to Diego Garcia during OIF. It seemed that no sooner had the bombers deployed than they had returned to Missouri, yet the effect that they had had on the battlefield was incalculable (USAF)

SPIRIT OF MISSOURI lifts off from the runway at Guam for another practice bombing mission in July 2005. The nose art and markings which are usually seen on other USAF aircraft are absent from the B-2As. They have an altogether more sober appearance which underlies their deadly mission (USAF)

Integration of the weapon with the B-2A has been eased by the fact that the aircraft did not need excessive modifications to be able to deploy it. Lt James Cole of the 419th Flight Test Squadron, who was responsible for the test in August, noted that 'there were no physical modifications done on the B-2 rotary launcher assembly. There was only a small software change made to the mission-independent data file in order to integrate the weapon onto the B-2'.

One month later, and the B-2A aircraft at Edwards was testing yet again – this time the integration of the GBU-82 bunker-busting JDAM onto the aircraft. These 500-lb bombs are amongst the smallest JDAM to be carried by the jet, allowing a Spirit to release 80 of them during a single bomb run. It took 11 sorties in total to qualify this weapon on the B-2A, and the tests were conducted using inert weapons.

The carriage of 80 such weapons gives the B-2 a bomb load more reminiscent of a World War 2 B-29 Superfortress or Cold War B-52H, but with one key difference – all of these bombs are guided munitions and, therefore, the Spirit may have a scattergun effect with such weapons, but this would be the equivalent of every pellet hitting its intended target. 419th FTS B-2A test pilot Maj William Power noted that 'the ability to strike 80 targets on one mission or, as demonstrated, on one bomb run, with incredible precision, immensely increased our operational capabilities'.

The aircraft required some minor modifications to be able to carry the internal smart bomb rack, and as with the GBU-28B/B weapon, some minor changes were also made to the jet's software to allow its computer to 'talk' to the JDAM. It was noted that there had been some initial concerns about dropping all 80 weapons in one go. Instead, the programme worked up towards dropping a full load of weapons, as Maj Power explained. 'There were some initial concerns about releasing 80 weapons in the time interval desired. To ensure the safety of the aircraft, we had to build up towards releasing the maximum number of JDAM'. Yet the testing regime did not finish with the September 2003 flight. The next stage was to then transition the entire programme to the 509th BW for installation and modification of the combat-coded B-2As, following the final tests of the software modifications for the aircraft.

No sooner had the B-2A performed its epic service in Iraq, than the 509th BW was back rehearsing its 'Global Power' deployments across the world. As well as operating from Diego Garcia, the aircraft can also be

deployed to Guam for operations in the Asian theatre. This is vital should any conflict with North Korea flare up. To this end, in September 2003, B-2As and their support personnel participated in Exercise *Coronet Dragon 49*. Ostensibly, the task of the exercise was to test the abilities of 509th BW units to forward-deploy to a location such as Guam and to be able to fight.

At the time, Lt Col Steve Basham was the Director of Operations at the 325th BS. He noted how important practice deployments to bases such as Diego Garcia and Guam are to the operational capabilities of the 509th BW;

'Exercises like this refine and maintain our ability to rapidly move air power assets anywhere in the world in response to national security needs as demonstrated in OIF. Forward basing allows a more rapid turnaround of aircraft, resulting in more missions against targets. This is a total force deployment exercise. Through the total force effort we can accomplish rapid and seamless mobility.'

Exercises such as this are not only important to the aircrews. They are also vital to the groundcrews, allowing them to practise operating at locations which are not necessarily familiar to them. Chief Master Sgt Raymond Reph of the 509th Aircraft Maintenance Squadron said that at the FOL 'we have minimal manning, equipment and supplies. When we deploy for real the airmen will be ready. Some day they will take my place and the Air Force needs them to be ready'.

SPIRIT OF MISSOURI and *SPIRIT OF OKLAHOMA* of the 13th and 393rd BSs, respectively, share ramp space at Andersen AFB in July 2005. Both aircraft have their undercarriage and crew doors open, and their serrated edges, which are necessary to reduce the radar signature of the aircraft, are clearly visible. Perforated spoilers in front of the bomb bays also help to control airflow during weapons release (*USAF*)

Interestingly, as with OIF, the 509th BW was effectively conducting simultaneous operations during *Coronet Dragon 49*, for not only were the jets participating in the exercise, they were also on station for the SIOP mission.

A similar deployment would take place in July 2005, when B-2s again went to Guam as the 393rd EBS. Spirits were deployed in what the DoD described as supporting 'Pacific Command's security efforts in the Western Pacific', which was presumably a reference as a deterrence and reassurance to US adversaries and allies in the area, *vis-à-vis* Japan, Thailand, Taiwan, the Philippines, Malaysia, Singapore and South Korea.

SPIRIT OF HAWAII of the 393rd BS sits on the ramp under guard at Guam. The regular deployments of the bombers to this Pacific island are as much of an exercise in reassurance to the United States' allies as they are a deterrence to its adversaries. The deployments are also essential for familiarising crews with the region (*USAF*)

It also sent a message to North Korea's Kim Yong Il that any attempt by him to use his nuclear weapons or to perpetrate aggression against his southern neighbour would be met with maximum force.

A total of 270 personnel left Whiteman for Guam, replacing the 93rd EBS and its B-52H aircraft which had deployed from Barksdale AFB, Louisiana. The US maintains a permanent bomber presence in this

The 13th BS's *SPIRIT OF WASHINGTON* moves down the taxiway at Guam in July 2005. The sunny weather betrays the high temperatures which both the aircraft and the personnel have to operate in. The environmentally controlled B2SS hangers go some way to reduce the climatic burdens on the aircraft, and thus help to reduce maintenance (*USAF*)

tinderbox neighbourhood, and for good measure. However, the deployment was not only intended to illustrate Washington's resolve, but to ensure that the B-2As can integrate fully with US Pacific Command's forces deployed in the area. This time, the jets were integrated into the 36th Expeditionary Operations Group. Its commander, Col Curtiss Petrek, noted that 'one of the things we do a lot with B-2 is fly missions that tend to be a lot longer than the average sorties that most of the aircraft fly. We'll get an opportunity to fly those missions and to really practise some of the command-and-control communications links'.

Part of the exercise was also aimed at familiarising aircrew with the peculiarities of flying from Andersen AFB. In much the same way that Missouri is some distance from the B-2As' targets, Guam is also a long way away from possible targets in the region. Col Petrek noted that 'the distances are so much further apart here, and if you are going to fly a mission, you need good command and control. It's important that everyone knows the systems you have, how they are to be used, and that they are used properly'.

Prior to this, it had been the B-52Hs which had formed the backbone of the US bomber punch in the region. This laid some good preparatory ground for the B-2A deployment, and the 93rd EBS had also helped with the 393rd EBS's exercise, as Col Petrek noted. 'The transition here has been pretty easy primarily because the prior B-52 unit deployed here worked with us well in advance to make our transition go smoothly'.

Practice JDAM rounds, recognisable by their blue nose cones, are delivered to *SPIRIT OF OKLAHOMA* during *Coronet Dragon 49*. The mix of JDAM and stealth has now become such a feature of US air power that Pentagon strategists could have been forgiven for wondering how on earth they managed to live without it (*USAF*)

Flying in formation with their F-15E counterparts, a B-2A glides through the Pacific skies during Exercise *Coronet Dragon 49* in July 2005 (*USAF*)

THE FUTURE

'It performed just the way we designed it to' was how James Kinnu summed up his feelings on how the B-2A fared in combat. 'All of us who were fully knowledgeable of its capabilities saw it being deployed just the way it was designed. The ability to fly from Whiteman AFB, to go "black" near the European continent and have everybody try to find it, but nobody doing so. Then having it accurately deliver weapons on target, including the Chinese Embassy, which was a mistake but not by the bomber, and the ability to do it under all weather conditions'. Irv Waaland agreed. 'It did what it was supposed to. It shut up the nay-sayers'.

GSConOps

The USAF has a bold new vision for how it expects to deploy its B-2A Spirits in the future. Stealthy F-22A Raptor air superiority fighters will protect groups of B-2As and F-117A as they fly towards their targets, firstly destroying fixed SAM sites housing systems such as the Russian-built S-300MPU/SA-10 (NATO codename 'Grumble'), S-300V/SA-12 'Giant' and S-400/SA-20 'Triumpf', along with their accompanying Command, Control and Communications (C^3) equipment. Along with the other aircraft, the Spirit's attentions will then focus on the high-value, fixed leadership targets and C^3 installations.

The mission of the aircraft will be to deliver a short, sharp shock to the enemy's military infrastructure, with the intention of rendering it incapable of retaliating against the forces which will flow into the theatre following the initial attacks. This collection of stealthy aircraft, coupled with sophisticated command and control systems, is known in USAF parlance as the Global Strike Concept of Operations (GSConOps) – it was formerly known as the Global Strike Task Force. Although it may sound like science fiction, GSConOps is, according to Col David Gerber, GSConOps 'champion' at the Pentagon's Directorate of Operational Capability Requirements, 'already up and running'.

The concept, in which the B-2A is a major component, takes lessons from history. During Operation *Desert Storm*, air power fragmented the command of Iraq's military machine and 'softened up' ground units in the field before the offensive to liberate Kuwait commenced. The campaign taught a vital lesson – allow the US and its allies sufficient time to build up their forces in the region and you will be promised, to quote a sign in the Pentagon during the campaign, an 'ass kicking of biblical proportions'. Deny access to your airspace, to bases on your doorstep, ports and troop assembly areas, maybe by fir-

A Lockheed Martin-built US Air Force F-22A Raptor fighter lands in front of a pair of Spirits at Nellis AFB during a recent *Red Flag* exercise. These two platforms are both major parts of the GSConOps initiative (*MSgt Michael R Nixion*)

SPIRIT OF KITTY HAWK prepares to touch down on the long main runway at Andersen AFB while two F/A-18C Hornets await their turn to take off during *Coronet Dragon 49* in July 2005 (*SRA Joshua Strang*)

ing ballistic missiles tipped with chemical or biological warheads, and US and allied forces will not have fixed locations from which to launch their assault.

The military build-up for *Desert Storm* took six months. Once combat began, erstwhile President Saddam Hussein did his best to deny the US-led Coalition access to his territory by firing modified R-300/ 9K72 Elbrus (SS-1 'Scud') missiles at Saudi Arabia, one of which killed 28 US military personnel after hitting a building on a US base in the desert Kingdom on 25 February 1991.

Mindful of this fact, and pre-empting the advent of GSConOps, Gen Charles A Horner, commander of the United States Central Command Air Forces during Operation *Desert Storm* told the US Congress in 1996 that, given the proliferation of ballistic missiles and WMD, it was imperative 'to shift as much of the power projection burden as we can – as fast as we can – to long range systems' such as the B-2A to avoid the need for third country basing.

To outflank such access denial strategies, and to enable US or Allied follow-on forces to defeat their enemy, USAF planners have designed GSConOps to play to the force's strengths – namely its ability to 'precisely employ mass firepower at global ranges', and to deploy low-visibility platforms such as the stealth bomber.

When air power was used during OAF, it was hoped that NATO bombing would persuade the Serbian leadership to, amongst other things, allow peacekeepers into Kosovo. As events turned out, it took longer for Belgrade to capitulate. The lesson learned was that the USAF might not have the luxury of deploying to, and mounting operations from, a neighbouring third country, as an adversary might seek to deny access to this territory by using ballistic missiles.

For the former Chief of the USAF's Air Combat Command, Gen John Jumper (the architect of GSConOps), OAF taught an important lesson. 'We should never start a limited operation if the enemy can turn it into a sustained conflict'.

With its engines idling, SPIRIT OF GEORGIA is just a few minutes away from departing Whiteman AFB and heading for Guam as part of *Coronet Dragon 49* (*SRA Tia Schroeder*)

Rather than conducting a graduated increase in bombing, such as that undertaken in Operation *Rolling Thunder* during the Vietnam War, the USAF will begin its air war with a sudden and focused bombing campaign similar to that seen during the dramatic 'Shock and Awe' attacks against Saddam Hussein's regime at the start of OIF, in which the B-2A played a key role.

According to Col Gerber, 'the whole (GSConOps) idea is pulled from the history of the last 50 years'. The use of the B-2A with precision weapons such as JDAM and the forthcoming Small Diameter Bomb (SDB) will allow USAF combat aircraft to outmanoeuvre their enemy. After all, why attack an enemy's strong points when you can smash its weak points?

Teaming up the B-2A with the F-22A in this role is known in USAF circles as the 'one-two punch'. During the first 24-hours of Operation *Desert Storm*, after six months of deploying to the region, the USAF hit 203 targets with 1223 attack sorties. GSConOps promises that four B-2As and 48 F-22As, armed with the forthcoming SDB precision munition, will be able to hit 380 targets in just 52 sorties. The Raptors and Spirits will not work alone. They will be supported by a focused electronic and information warfare campaign that will render the enemy's C³ lines useless and leave their computer and radar screens blank.

An all-out surgical attack against an enemy's air defences, C³ lines and leadership will, Gen Jumper hopes, give the adversary 'an excuse to quit' and throw in the towel early, saving time and lives. This will be a break from the past as previously, 'we weren't able to do the job with a shock attack. It took persistent 24-hour-a-day operations over the battlefield for a sustained period of time to get the job done'.

Rather than hitting massed formations of troops in the field, surrounded by heavy air defences, the C³ nervous systems which control these forces will be attacked, paralysing the enemy early on in the fight. Gen Jumper is confident that 'stealth applied to bombers and manoeuvrable fighters, all-weather precision-guided munitions (PGMs), and unmanned aerial vehicles (UAVs) will allow us to manoeuvre over, around and through – or to stand-off outside the advanced defensive systems and networks already available to potential adversaries'.

Inert Small Diameter Bombs are loaded into the bomb-bay of a B-2A. The advent of the weapon will give the bomber yet more destructive power and allow the Spirit to bring yet more capability to the fight (*Boeing*)

The 412th TW's B-2 *SPIRIT OF NEW YORK* drops 32 inert 500-lb GBU-38 JDAM on the Utah Testing and Training Range near Hill AFB on 27 August 2004 (*USAF*)

It is hoped that GSConOps will provide the 'maximum shock during the first stage of the battle'. Such a display might even persuade an adversary that 'resistance is futile' and encourage them to sue for peace, rather than endure more attacks. Col Gerber stresses that 'the point of strategy and war is to force the adversary to change their mind'. Moreover, the stealthy qualities of the Raptors, Spirits and Nighthawks will be all but impossible to defend against.

Before the opening strikes, all-weather sensors, based on aircraft such as the E-8C, the RQ-4 Global Hawk UAV and satellites will closely watch the prospective area of operations to identify targets which are to be destroyed early such as fixed SAM sites, command and control installations, leadership targets and WMDs.

The initial attack will be sudden and swift, mixing stealth with high-speed, precision and up-to-the-second information on enemy strengths and targets. The spearhead of the GSConOps force will be the F-22A Raptor, which will also escort the B-2As. These aircraft will strike additional high-value SAM, C^3 and WMD targets with precision weapons. A major priority for the force will be to destroy the enemy's so-called 'double-digit' SAMs.

Destroying the fixed SAM sites will open a corridor for further waves of attack aircraft. Hitting key C^3 facilities should also help to prevent an adversary distributing orders to their armed forces to counter the USAF offensive. Destroying ballistic, cruise or anti-shipping missile sites will help to prevent any attacks on other US forces which might be massing near the theatre of operations.

A typical GSConOps attack would begin with a brace of B-2As, F-117As and F-22s entering enemy airspace, while B-52H bombers armed with cruise missiles will loiter beyond the enemy's borders. Between them, they will deliver a devastating initial attack against the enemy's fixed SAM sites and C^3 installations. Meanwhile, the Raptors will defend the bombers should the enemy's air force try to engage.

With the initial attacks complete, the Spirits will begin combat air patrols in a 'cab rank', waiting for orders to attack time-critical and fixed targets as they are identified by reconnaissance aircraft. Meanwhile, missile-armed UAVs will engage heavily fortified targets which present too much of a threat to the crewed aircraft. Once the initial strike is complete and the anti-aircraft threat has been degraded, follow-on formations of less stealthy aircraft such as the F-35 Joint Strike Fighter and the US Navy's F/A-18E/F Super Hornet will conduct precision attacks from around 15,000 ft on, or around, the third day of the conflict.

GSConOps is designed to eliminate many of the challenges seen in recent air operations involving US forces. It will do away with the need for overseas air bases on the doorstep of an adversary such as those used in Saudi Arabia, Bahrain and the United Arab Emirates during Operation *Desert Storm*. The precision weapons that the force will employ will help to minimise civilian casualties and collateral damage on the ground. The stealthiness of the principal aircraft types involved will render it largely invulnerable to air-to-air and SAM threats, while a relatively small force will be able to inflict a level of damage far outstripping its size.

Advanced C^3 systems will allow time-critical targets to be struck, while keeping an eagle-eye on the battlefield, and the skies above it. Finally, the all-weather capabilities of the force will mean that the poor meteorological conditions which were seen during Operations *Desert Storm*, *Allied Force* and *Iraqi Freedom* should not have such an impact on the war effort.

The Spirits will also benefit from new climate-controlled hangers which have been built at the USAF FOLs at Diego Garcia and RAF Fairford. This will give additional bases from where the B-2A can operate.

The SDB is scheduled to enter service this year, whilst the F-22A Raptor started reaching the 1st Fighter Wing in 2005 and the Joint Strike Fighter is schedule to begin its USAF service in 2008.

However, questions must now be asked as to whether there are enough Spirits to perform both GSConOps and other USAF tasks. At present, the USAF has just 21 B-2As, of which only 18 are 'combat coded' – i.e. fit for combat operations. There has been much debate in recent years about reactivating the B-2A production line. In 1996, the former US Deputy Secretary of Defense, Dr Paul Wolfowitz, noted that 'future aggressors may draw a lesson from the Gulf War and attack nearby bases from the outset. In those circumstances, additional B-2 bombers, operating from bases beyond the reach of enemy missiles or aircraft would be valuable'. However, once Dr Wolfowitz became firmly ensconced in the Pentagon, there was precious little further comment about restarting the Spirit production line.

Present estimates talk of the aircraft remaining in service until 2030, although some analysts believe that it will be retired sooner given its maintenance requirements. However, this is disputed by those who work with the aircraft, particularly at the maintenance level.

'Right now, we make statements like "it'll be here through 2030". The folks that maintain it – from the NCOs to the senior NCOs that have worked on a number of different aircraft, both bombers and fighters – say this aircraft is probably the most solidly built jet they've ever worked on. In terms of its structure, this aircraft has much more in common with a fighter than it does with a bomber. It's a very strong, very rigid aircraft. It has a powerful airframe. Since it's mainly non-metal, we do corrosion control on the aircraft, but the corrosion is not nearly the problem on composite aircraft as it is on aluminium aircraft', noted a B-2 crew chief.

One of the most important debates regarding the B-2A is whether additional aircraft will be manufactured. Original estimates for the Spirit's production run talked of over 100 aircraft being produced, but this was eventually reduced, given political disagreements, to the 21 aircraft which the USAF currently possesses. Nevertheless, a debate has lingered since the aircraft's entry into service about whether the Northrop Grumman production line should be reactivated for additional aircraft to be delivered.

At the nub of the debate is the issue that, given the low number of aircraft which were originally purchased, the unit cost for each jet was dramatically high. This is because of a simple economy of scale – the more you build of something, the cheaper its price becomes. Suffice to say that the aircraft's critics called the Spirit the 'two billion dollar blunder', and any future bomber is now expected to be fantastically expensive. Therefore, it is perhaps no coincidence that several industry and USAF studies into the future of bombers discuss an unmanned alternative to the current manned bomber fleet.

Yet there is a strong faction in the Air Force that insists on a manned bomber being necessary, and that technology for an unmanned system is not yet sufficiently matured to a point where the latter would be as flexible and responsive as the former. Cynics say that this argument has arisen because USAF pilots do not want to vote themselves out of a job.

Therefore, surely one way out of building a very expensive B-2A replacement could be simply to build more B-2As? During the 2000 US Presidential election campaign, Donald H Rumsfeld and Richard Cheney, who would go on to become Defense Secretary and Vice President respectively in the Admin-

B-2A aircrew return from their aircraft, having completed a training mission during Guam deployment in July 2005. At the moment, the aircraft has two crew members. Will bombers in the future have zero? (Ted Carlson)

istration of President George W Bush, publicly supported calls for stealth bomber production to resume, but these calls so far have remained just that, and nothing more has been said on the subject by the two men since they took up their appointments.

Prior to this, Bush's predecessor, Bill Clinton had been lobbied hard by five former defence secretaries – Melvin Laird, James Schlesinger, Harold Brown, Casper Weinberger and Frank Carlucci – about building more B-2As. They argued that the aircraft 'remains the most cost-effective means of rapidly projecting force over great distances. Its range enables it to reach any point on earth within hours after launch while being deployed at only three secure bases around the world. Its payload and array of munitions will permit it to destroy numerous time-sensitive targets in a single sortie. And perhaps most importantly, its LO characteristics will allow it to reach intended targets without fear of interception. It is already apparent that the end of the Cold War was neither the end of history nor the end of danger. We hope it also will not be the end of the B-2'.

Evidently the Clinton administration had other priorities. For James Kinnu, the problem is that not enough bombers were built in the first place. 'I think that the United States, as will all of the free world, regret that they didn't build a lot more of them'.

But simply restarting production is not that simple. Studies by Northrop Grumman have shown that reopening the B-2A production line to deliver 40 new aircraft would cost at least $29.4 billion, or $735 million per aircraft. This is still not that cheap when one takes into account that the projected FB-22A medium-bomber variant of the Lockheed Martin F-22 Raptor will cost around $100 million per airframe. This figure also includes the cost of reopening the B-2 production line, which could be expected to total $4 billion alone.

Moreover, these projected new Spirits would not be facsimiles of their older siblings. Northrop Grumman say that they would be so-called 'Charlie' variants, unable to perform nuclear missions in order to save money due to their lack of equipment hardening them against the Electro-Magnetic Pulse (EMP) that accompanies a nuclear explosion. They would instead be solely configured for conventional operations. This begs the question as to what is the rationale of building such an expensive aircraft which is confined to a conventional mission, given that it would not be outfitted with equipment to protect itself against the EMP. Why not spend the extra cash and get an 'all-singing, all-bombing' platform instead?

The other issue in building new B-2s, whether A- or C-models, is that there is not a massively pressing requirement for them by the USAF at the moment. As we have seen, the B-2A has proved itself beyond doubt in recent conflicts, but at the same time these conflicts have not illustrated that more aircraft are desperately needed. Even in a high-tempo aerial campaign such as that witnessed during OAF, the jet was able to demonstrate that it could meet the required tasking while maintaining its SIOP responsibilities, and that was with just one operational squadron.

In essence, the USAF has been able to perform the number of Spirit missions that it wants to with the number of bombers that it has. Furthermore, in the highly political world of US defence procurement, the Spirit production line reactivation lobby will also have to compete with existing and forthcoming programmes such as the KC-135 replacement, F-22, F-35 Joint Strike Fighter and the Combat Search and Rescue helicopter replacement. All of these initiatives are equally vital programmes, and it would be hard to see how lawmakers could reduce or cancel one at the expense of buying more versions of an aircraft which is already in service.

Also, the B-2A is not the only bomber in USAF service, with the more numerous B-52H and B-1B also shouldering the bombing burden. They are perfectly adequate for performing bombing missions once the air defence threat has been swept aside. B-1Bs have the added benefit, thanks to their defensive aids suite, of being able to operate in high-risk areas. The B-2A's strength is as a specialist and not a generalist aircraft, and for this reason fewer may be needed.

However, Northrop Grumman has maintained its efforts to get Spirit production restarted following the commencement of George W Bush's tenure. Perceived as an altogether more 'defence friendly' administration than the preceding one, the company was no doubt hopeful that the Pentagon might give the green light for more aircraft. Northrop Grumman Chief Executive Kent Kresa wrote to Donald Rumsfeld saying that the production line could be reactivated in 2003, and that production of the aircraft could continue until 2016.

Despite the high cost estimations of resuming production, the company argued that savings would be possible. Despite not having 'nuke-proof' avionics, the aircraft would enjoy more modern avionics than those of the 1970s vintage which were installed in the original. These would be cheaper to operate because they would require less mainte-nance. Moreover, the aircraft's all-important coatings and materials would be more modern, hardier and hence cheaper, as they would require less frequent maintenance

Despite the seemingly matt finish of the aircraft's skin, a close-up shot of SPIRIT OF LOUISIANA illustrates the varied and discoloured appearance of the aircraft where its RAMs have been repaired (*Ted Carlson*)

and replacement. Finally, the airframe is already a proven aerodynamic concept, and therefore would not require an expensive test regime to prove that the design actually flies.

The most conservative estimates talk of the aircraft leaving service in 2024, given that the jet was designed for a 30-year service life. The initial Developmental Test and Evaluation analysis performed by the USAF for the B-2A estimated that the structural life of the aircraft should be good for around 40,000 flight hours based on anticipated usage and flight profiles. The problem is that the USAF will have to start thinking quickly if it is to have a replacement aircraft by 2024.

In order to ensure a smooth transition to the new bombing platform, assuming that the USAF decides to procure a B-2 replacement, then such an aircraft would have to be ready to enter service around 2017. This presents the USAF with a dilemma. State-of-the-art military aircraft now take decades to produce. The stealth bomber passed through almost two decades from its inception to entry into service.

In Europe, the Eurofighter Typhoon and the Dassault Rafale went through similarly protracted gestations before they arrived on the flightline. Even if the USAF began work on the Spirit replacement tomorrow, it would only have ten years to field a new aircraft which could do all the B-2's missions and more. You can bet your bottom dollar that such a project would initially encounter heavy political debate over cost and necessity before the first metal was even cut. Moreover, as recent high-ticket aircraft projects, such as those listed above, have shown, the project would almost certainly be late and over budget – that is if it escapes the budgetary axe in the current climate of heightened scrutiny of ever-increasing defence costs.

Does this not lead us back to the unmanned debate? Why not simply get an armed UAV to do the job of the stealth bomber? There is a simple answer to this. Broadly speaking, developing an unmanned version of the stealth bomber would not be cheap either. Much of the technology in terms of autonomous flight is still in its infancy and under development. Secondly, there are very real legal debates about using an unmanned combat aircraft for air strikes. For example, who is responsible if a bomb goes awry and hits the kindergarten and not the command centre? The operator, the manufacturer, the politicians or the soldier flying the aircraft thousands of miles away? Secondly, would the air force, the general public and the politicians feel comfortable placing nuclear weapons on a pilotless aircraft?

There is final question about the B-2A's future. At the time of writing the aircraft has never experienced any losses. Lose one B-2A and you lose around five percent of the force. Lose four and 25 percent of the fleet is destroyed. Any losses of these aircraft would be keenly felt, as it is the only stealth aircraft which can fly prolonged missions to anywhere in the world from the United States with such a large weapons payload.

The efforts of the maintainers and the personnel who work with the B-2 to ensure that it is kept in top condition are beyond doubt, but aircraft are like people, and the older they get, the more care they need and the more maintenance they require. One theory states that as the aircraft mature, they will require more maintenance as components get tired and increase the bomber's systems failure rates. This could mean that at any single point, up to five aircraft are out of service undergoing deep maintenance, leaving around 14 aircraft (given that one airframe is based at Edwards AFB with the 412th TW for evaluation and test flights) to perform SIOP and conventional missions.

Furthermore, some estimates have predicted that one aircraft will be lost for every ten years of service. This is based upon the service life of the B-52. What happens then if the nightmare scenario of two major wars involving the US flare up simultaneously and over a quarter of the B-2 fleet is in deep maintenance?

IMPROVEMENTS AND UPGRADES

James Kinnu believes that there will be further improvements to the aircraft throughout the rest of its life. 'There'll be upgrades to the avionics, and I think that there will be upgrades in the LO technology area, particularly as it relates to the materials being used on the jet. There'll be new weapons which the aircraft is qualified to use over time'.

However, in the short term work continues to ensure that the aircraft stays responsive and razor-sharp. One aspect of this is ensuring that the training aids used by the aircrew are the best and the most up-to-date possible. To this end, in May 2003 the Link Simulation and Training division of L3 Communications was awarded a $22.07 million delivery order for the company to develop 'concurrency upgrades' to the B-2A training systems used by the aircrews and the maintainers. These improvements will ensure that the training systems accurately mirror the aircraft, taking into account any of the improvements and upgrades which the B-2A has benefited from.

Central to these improvements were changes made to the aircraft mission, maintenance and weapons load trainers which took into account the Link-16-based Center Instrument Display/In-Flight Replanning System which is currently being installed in the B-2 fleet. It is essential that all personnel working with the jet are fully conversant with the Link-16 system, as this is a vital tactical datalink which connects the B-2A to other US and allied aircraft, and command centres, allowing the Spirit to receive updates to its mission while in-flight.

Known as the Multifunction Information Datalink System (MIDS), this Link-16-based system will enter service with the B-2A community this year. It is one of a host of improvements that the aircraft will obtain. Other additions include the Beyond Line of Sight (BLOS) communications system, which replaces the existing radios in the aircraft along with the present satellite communications (SATCOM) system. Upgrades to the aircraft's computer are also on the cards.

The rapid pace with which defence computing is accelerating means that several of the computing components which were initially fitted to the B-2A are no longer manufactured, thus making spare parts increasingly more difficult to find. Moreover, new systems are more efficient, and also provide more computing power. With the B-2, this translates into vital improvements to the aircraft's offensive and defensive avionics systems.

Crucially, these improvements will also enable the aircraft to carry a mixed weapons load-out, which translates into a wider variety of missions that the B-2A can successfully execute. GBU-31s and GBU-28 'bunker busters' on the same aircraft mean that a B-2A can hit a SCUD missile launcher in the field and then go on to destroy its hardened command centre. In the

GSConOps was to take both the B-2A and the F-117A well into the next decade, although the recent announcement that the latter type will be retired in 2008 may change these plans. The jets were to be used together with their forthcoming counterparts to punch a hole through sophisticated air defence systems for the entry of follow-on forces. Despite the B-2A being a Cold War weapon, GSConOps illustrates that it is now an essential military system for today and tomorrow's world (*USAF*)

The B-2A bomber has been the recipient of a steady stream of upgrades intended to keep its talons sharp despite changes in global threats (*Ted Carlson*)

cockpit, aircrew will get modern Liquid Crystal Display (LCD)-type screens, replacing the more antiquated Cathode Ray Tube displays.

For the crews, the cockpit will also gain Digital Engine Controllers to replace the original analogue controllers, which were classified as 'high failure items'. The replacement of these components will improve the B-2's performance, while also boosting its maintainability and making it easier to support. The speed of the jet's responsiveness will also be accelerated through the installation of a fibre-optic databus which allows more information to be transferred faster from the B-2's avionics to its weapons, while at the same time being more robust to the EMP.

One of the most important components in the B-2A is its AN/APQ-181 radar. This is scheduled to be improved under the Radar Modernization Program. This will see an Active Electronically Scanned Array (AESA) improvement to the aircraft's existing system, with testing of the new equipment commencing in 2007. The contract, which was awarded in 2004, is to install an AESA radar system which uses a grid of so-called 'smart transmit-receive elements' that can either work together on a specific radar task or perform different functions. This is known in the trade as 'scan here,

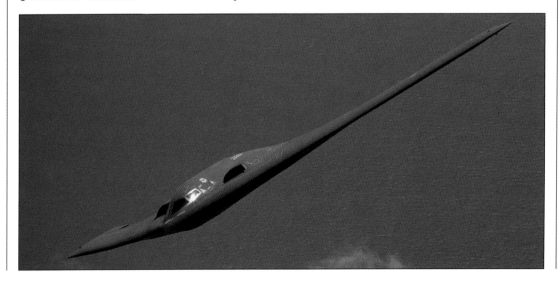

while track there'. This is an important addition, as it would allow the B-2A's radar to watch two different areas of interest, and to change its targeting priorities accordingly, should the radar notice something new such as a convoy of surface-to-surface missile Transporter Erector Launchers, emerging from a military facility. The Link-16 system would allow the bomber to then transfer details of this targeting change to other aircraft and command centres.

At the same time, the Spirit will also get enhancements to manage its all-important radar signature. This is

vital because air defence threats are continually evolving. America's existing and potential adversaries are well aware of the aircraft's capabilities, and threats to counter the B-2A cannot be expected to remain static. To this end, research efforts constantly seek out ways to reduce the aircraft's radar signature and to enhance the Spirit's physical and electronic defences. The USAF remains understandably quiet about what these initiatives are, although they are expected to focus on the aircraft's structural materials, tactical procedures and support equipment.

Following the completion of the Block 30 upgrade to the B-2 fleet, improvements were made to the jet's RAMs to further enhance the aircraft's survivability. The new coating had the net effect of reducing the aircraft's maintenance time per flight hour from almost 21 hours to just over nine – a saving of more than 50 percent. Before these improvements, maintainers had to cover the edges of access panels, which would reflect radar energy and hence risk betraying the bomber's position, with RAM tape. The improved system did away with the tape, which often had the added risk of coming loose in flight. Instead, a special RAM coating, which absorbs radar energy as it penetrates the cracks on the aircraft's surfaces, was applied to the edges

Weapons Loading Technicians from the 509th Aircraft Maintenance Squadron install safety pins to secure the JSOW in a B-2A during *Coronet Dragon 49*. This weapon is one of many new systems designed to give the aircraft more punch as it moves through the 21st century (*SRA Tia C Schroeder*)

Backlit by a stunning Pacific sunset, the sleek shape of the B-2A has given it a timeless beauty. Thoughts are now turning to what will replace the Spirit, be it manned or unmanned (*Ted Carlson*)

SPIRIT OF OHIO is bathed in the moonlight at Andersen AFB while being readied for a training mission from the Pacific Island (*SSgt Bennie J Davis III*)

of the access doors. The USAF notes that work on improving the aircraft's coating is ongoing, constantly evolving to further reduce the aircraft's signature.

In terms of weaponry, the B-2A literally has 'room for improvement'. The airframe contains two storage bays on either side of the main undercarriage wells which are around nine feet long and as deep as the aircraft's wing. Originally, it was planned that these boxes would house an exhaust suppression system which would dilute the aircraft's contrails with chemicals to make them difficult to see with the naked eye.

As things turned out, these bays were never used, and instead thought is now being given to using this space as surrogate weapons bays to house small-sized cruise missiles, giving the aircraft yet more punch. USAF planners envisage these missiles being used for counter-air defence strikes against radars, or maybe to house decoy equipment and jamming systems which could further protect the aircraft, much in the same way that the ADM-20 Quail electronic decoy did for the B-52.

In terms of weaponry improvements, the aircraft is scheduled to obtain the Enhanced GBU-28, known as the EGBU-28, which will replace the earlier GBU-37 hard target penetrating weapon. Boasting GPS-enhanced accuracy, it is said that this weapon can penetrate more than 100 ft of soft ground or 20 ft of concrete. Other improvements include the AGM-158 Joint Air to Surface Stand-off Missile (JASSM), which gives the aircraft the capability to perform attacks from a stand-off range of 200 miles from the target. This weapon also carries a 1000-lb warhead. Finally, the 500-lb GBU-38 JDAM will also be deployed on the B-2A. This will give the Spirit a near mythical bomb load of 80 such PGMs, almost turning the aircraft into a 'one-aeroplane strike force'.

Sgt Beau Turner is confident about the capability that the GBU-38 will bring to the aircraft;

'This aircraft has such an awesome capability. In OIF our munitions capability was 16 weapons per jet with the 2000-lb JDAM. We can now drop 80 500-lb weapons which we can independently target. That is an awesome capability. That's something that we didn't have at the beginning of OIF. Every year, we increase our capability more and more. We're always looking for different munitions to carry. When you look at the B-2 there's a lot of things that you don't think about. The jet has an awesome targeting capability, whether it be flexible targeting or whatever the case maybe. There's a lot of stuff that we can do in the air.

'We can take off from CONUS thinking that we're going to do this one thing and we end up doing something completely different based on the fact that the battlefield scenario has changed. And to be able to go to a capability where we can drop 80 independent weapons is awesome. The SDB is one of the capabilities which we are looking at, and I think that the last number I heard was something like 200+ that we'd be able to drop. We've heard anywhere between 160 and 240. I don't really know what the exact number is, but I'm sure all that will be worked out.'

The SDB is a key USAF programme, and two versions are under development. One will have a terminal seeker and target recognition head and the other will be guided by either a GPS or an inertial navigation system. Both variants will have a 250-lb warhead.

For Lt Col Steve Basham, the increased bomb load will also be warmly welcomed by the aircrew;

'Like the B-1 and the B-52, the B-2 will be able to carry a large load of SDBs. This makes us just a little bit different from smaller strike aircraft because we can actually plan to hit many different targets during the course of a single sortie. Every conflict prior to now, we've carried the 2000-lb JDAM as our weapon of choice, but with the GBU-38 available to us, we will now have a truly phenomenal force-multiplying capability. Eighty different weapons to go against 80 independently-targeted desired points of intercept will give our our "vault" (Mission Planning Cell) far greater options.'

Will the B-2A be the last manned bomber? James Kinnu believes 'that's a hard question to answer. Obviously, the technology has come a lot further since we finished. I'm quite confident that there is the capability available to design a supersonic bomber if there is a need for one. If it was unmanned, it would be a lot easier to design, for when you put a man in it, it gets bigger'.

The effect that the B-2A has had on the USAF in particular, and global warfare in general, has been profound. Lt Col Thomas Bussiere, 13th BS Commander, is in no doubt about its impact. 'Obviously no one wishes for war, but when war comes, I want to be in a B-2 to send the message that the United States is ready to deal with the task at hand. A B-2 with its capability will only put two crew members at risk versus four or more – that's the right thing to do. Wrap it all up into the weapons systems and I'd be lying if I didn't tell you that everyone stands with pride at Whiteman AFB when we're called to task, and I think that holds true for the nation too'.

Deployed for another *Red Flag* exercise, the destructive power which can be wielded by this trio of machines is staggering. Two aircraft alone could have performed the 1986 Operation *Eldorado Canyon* against Libya with little in the way of supporting assets (*MSgt Michael R Nixon*)

APPENDICES

B-2A FLEET LIST

Both the 13th and 393rd BSs, together with the 394th CTS, have no B-2As permanently assigned to them according to Capt Adam Cuquet of the 394th. 'We have so many down for maintenance and upgrades that we pretty much share each other's jets, whereas in the B-1 community your squadron has its own aircraft. So many unexpected things happen with engines out or systems maintenance that we pretty much share them all'.

Air Vehicle Number	Northrop Grumman Build Serial Number	USAF Serial Number	Block (when delivered)	Official Name	Delivery Date
AV-1	1001	82-1066	Block 30	SPIRIT OF AMERICA	January 2000
AV-2	1002	82-1067	Block 30	SPIRIT OF ARIZONA	4/12/97
AV-3	1003	82-1068	Block 30	SPIRIT OF NEW YORK	10/10/97
AV-4	1004	82-1069	Block 30	SPIRIT OF INDIANA	22/5/99
AV-5	1005	82-1070	Block 20	SPIRIT OF OHIO	18/7/97
AV-6	1006	82-1071	Block 30	SPIRIT OF MISSISSIPPI	23/5/97
AV-7	1007	88-0328	Block 10	SPIRIT OF TEXAS	31/8/94
AV-8	1008	88-0329	Block 10	SPIRIT OF MISSOURI	31/3/94
AV-9	1009	88-0330	Block 10	SPIRIT OF CALIFORNIA	17/8/94
AV-10	1010	88-0331	Block 10	SPIRIT OF SOUTH CAROLINA	30/12/94
AV-11	1011	88-0332	Block 10	SPIRIT OF WASHINGTON	29/10/94
AV-12	1012	89-0127	Block 10	SPIRIT OF KANSAS	17/2/95
AV-13	1013	89-0128	Block 10	SPIRIT OF NEBRASKA	28/6/95
AV-14	1014	89-0129	Block 10	SPIRIT OF GEORGIA	14/11/95
AV-15	1015	90-0040	Block 10	SPIRIT OF ALASKA	24/1/96
AV-16	1016	90-0041	Block 10	SPIRIT OF HAWAII	10/1/96
AV-17	1017	92-0700	Block 20	SPIRIT OF FLORIDA	3/7/96
AV-18	1018	93-1085	Block 20	SPIRIT OF OKLAHOMA	15/5/96
AV-19	1019	93-1086	Block 20	SPIRIT OF KITTY HAWK	30/8/96
AV-20	1020	93-1087	Block 30	SPIRIT OF PENNSYLVANIA	5/8/97
AV-21	1021	93-1088	Block 30	SPIRIT OF LOUISIANA	10/11/97

COLOUR PLATES

1
B-2A 93-1087 *SPIRIT OF PENNSYLVANIA*, 393rd BS/ 509th BW, Whiteman AFB, September 1997
SPIRIT OF PENNSYLVANIA was the 15th B-2 delivered and the first Block 30 aircraft to arrive at Whiteman. The jet was named during a ceremony at Willow Grove Reserve Air Station in Philadelphia, having been directly flown there from the Northrop Grumman manufacturing facility at Palmdale. Arriving in Philadelphia on 7 August 1997, the bomber departed for Whiteman two days later. On 6 November that year it performed a test drop of inert JDAM at the Utah Test Range. On 9 March 1998 93-1087 expended the first ever load of Mk 82 500-lb bombs to be dropped from a B-2, the ordnance hitting an island at the Faradon range in the Pacific Ocean. The aircraft's nose gear door (see page 62) is notable for its absence of crew names, painted over in the interests of security and the nine mission markings.

2
B-2A 93-1086 *SPIRIT OF KITTY HAWK*, 13th BS/ 509th BW, Whiteman AFB, October 2005
SPIRIT OF KITTY HAWK was the 13th B-2 to be delivered to the 509th BW, and the third Block 20 aircraft built. It arrived at Whiteman on 30 August 1996, but was not named until 17 December, when a christening ceremony for the aircraft took place on the 52nd anniversary of the founding of the 509th BW. The unit was known as the 509th Composite Wing when formed, and led by a certain Col Paul Tibbets. The actions of the wing in August 1945 arguably made the unit the most famous in the USAAF. The aircraft was named during a ceremony at Seymour Johnson AFB in North Carolina.

3
B-2A 90-0041 *SPIRIT OF HAWAII*, 393rd BS/ 509th BW, Whiteman AFB, February 1996
SPIRIT OF HAWAII was the ninth Block 10 aircraft to be delivered, arriving at Whiteman on 10 January 1996. If 50 B-2As had been constructed, it would have been possible to name each aircraft after a state in the Union. After all, it has been claimed that components and subsystems for the jet are manufactured in every state! Nineteen of the twenty-one B-2As are named after states.

4
B-2A 88-0329 *SPIRIT OF MISSOURI*, 13th BS/ 509th BW, Whiteman AFB, September 2005
SPIRIT OF MISSOURI was the third stealth bomber to be delivered to Whiteman, the aircraft arriving at the base on 31 August 1994. It was reported that the jet made an appearance at the 'Wings over Houston' airshow on 20-21 October 2001, performing its flypast as it returned from a mission over Afghanistan. The cheers from the crowd were said to have drowned out the engine noise of the bomber as it overflew Ellington Field.

5
B-2A 82-1071 *SPIRIT OF MISSISSIPPI*, 325th BS/ 509th BW, Whiteman AFB, October 2001
The 19th B-2A to be delivered, and the first Block 30 aircraft, this jet was given the unofficial nickname the *Black Widow*. The bomber was given its official name during a ceremony at Jackson Air National Guard Base in Mississippi. Along with *SPIRIT OF LOUISIANA*, this jet was one of the first into battle during OEF when it performed a 43.5-hour sortie from Whiteman on 6 October 2001. It returned home to Missouri on the 8th following a crew change in Diego Garcia.

6
B-2A 82-1070 *SPIRIT OF OHIO*, 393rd BS/509th BW, Whiteman AFB, January 1997
SPIRIT OF OHIO was the 14th Spirit to be delivered, and the fourth Block 20 aircraft. The jet participated in several temperature testing evaluations during its early years in service. In 1993, it underwent 1000 hours of temperature testing at McKinley Climate Laboratory at Eglin AFB, Florida, during which it experienced temperatures of between 45 and 120 degrees Fahrenheit. The jet's performance at the other end of the temperature spectrum was evaluated three years later during a deployment to Eielson AFB, Alaska. It is perhaps no surprise, therefore, that the aircraft earned the nickname *FIRE & ICE*, which was painted onto its nose gear door. The latter was given to the USAF Museum at Wright-Patterson AFB for attachment to the collection's B-2 static test airframe.

7
B-2A 89-0127 *SPIRIT OF KANSAS*, 393rd BS/ 509th BW, Whiteman AFB, July 1997
The sixth Block 10 aircraft delivered, *SPIRIT OF KANSAS* was issued to the 509th on 18 February 1995. The aircraft performed the wing's first ever mission over the Pacific Ocean when it flew to the Hawaiian Islands to mark the 50th anniversary of VJ-Day on 1 September that same year. In 1997, this aircraft performed the first ever mission of a B-2A to the UK when it conducted a flypast at the Royal International Air Tattoo at RAF Fairford. As usual with all B-2As visiting the UK, the jet was escorted by two F-15Es from the 48th FW at RAF Lakenheath.

8
B-2A 93-1085 *SPIRIT OF OKLAHOMA*, 393rd BS/ 509th BW, Whiteman AFB, December 1998
SPIRIT OF OKLAHOMA was the 11th aircraft to be delivered to Whiteman, and the first Block 20 machine. The 509th would perform its first Block 20 sortie with this jet on 1 June 1996, and two-and-a-half years later, on 8 January 1999, this aircraft would be the last Block 20 airframe to leave Whiteman for Palmdale. There, it was modified to Block 30 status, after which the bomber became one of the first B-2s to see combat in OEF.

9
B-2A 82-1066 *SPIRIT OF AMERICA*, 393rd BS/ 509th BW, Whiteman AFB, October 2001
The brazenly patriotic *Spirit of America* was the last B-2A to be delivered, in Block 30 form, in early 2000. Perhaps it was quite fitting that *SPIRIT OF AMERICA* was also one of the first bombers to see combat in OEF. The aircraft logged a 44.3-hour sortie and went into action alongside the *SPIRIT OF GEORGIA*, which flew for just over 40 hours. Interestingly, this aircraft now shares its name with an F-22A Raptor which rolled off the Lockheed Martin production line at Marietta, Georgia, on 9 April 1997 – just eight days after the 509th received its initial operating capability. The nose gear door of *SPIRIT OF AMERICA* had patriotic artwork applied to it (see page 62) in the wake of the 11 September 2001 attacks, as did many other USAF and US Navy aircraft.

10
B-2A 82-1068 *SPIRIT OF NEW YORK*, 410th TS/ 412th TW, Edwards AFB, January 1996
Serving with the 410th TS at Edwards AFB, *SPIRIT OF NEW YORK* was the first Block 30 aircraft built. Another jet with its fair share of nicknames, it has been called *Navigator, Ghost* and *Afternoon Delight*! It is the only B-2A which is located at Edwards AFB. One of the luminaries to fly the aircraft with the 410th TS is Lt Col Michael T Good, who is scheduled to be a Mission Specialist for an up and coming Space Shuttle flight, having trained with the National Aeronautics and Space Administration as an Astronaut. Lt Col Good was a B-2A test pilot, flying the *SPIRIT OF NEW YORK*, between 1994 and 1997.

11
B-2A 89-0128 *SPIRIT OF NEBRASKA*, 393rd BS/509th BW, Whiteman AFB, September 1995
The seventh aircraft to be delivered to Whiteman was the *SPIRIT OF NEBRASKA*, which was the seventh Block 10 B-2 built. The jet arrived at Whiteman on 28 June 1995, but it was not named until a ceremony was held at Offutt AFB, Nebraska, several months later. Offutt was the home of Strategic Air Command – an outfit synonymous with the Cold War and America's nuclear deterrent. No sooner had the B-2A entered service than SAC was disbanded on 2 June 1992. Ironically, SAC never saw its most advanced aircraft serve under its command and instead the B-1B was dubbed 'SAC's last bomber'. On the same day that the *SPIRIT OF NEBRASKA* was named, two of the 509th's T-38 Talons were christened *SPIRIT OF WARRENSBURG* and *SPIRIT OF SEDALIA*.

12
B-2A 90-0040 *SPIRIT OF ALASKA*, 393rd BS/ 509th BW, Whiteman AFB, March 1996
SPIRIT OF ALASKA was the tenth aircraft to be delivered to Whiteman. The jet's arrival on 10 January 1996 was a highly significant event, as it marked the halfway point in the raising of the 509th's bomber force. The aircraft was also one of the Spirits to make the voyage across the 'Pond' to events in England when, in 2000, it was part of the static display at RAF Mildenhall for that year's Air Fete.

13
B-2A 88-0328 *SPIRIT OF TEXAS*, 393rd BS/509th BW, Whiteman AFB, February 1996
This aircraft was nicknamed *Pirate Ship* as well as having its official title as a tribute to the Lone Star State. Interestingly, this nickname, like all of those given to the early B-2As, fell out of use once the jet had been given its official moniker, and the Spirits have not inherited the tradition of obtaining highly individual and characteristic names as bestowed on their B-1B and B-52 brethren. The Flag Patch for this aircraft, like many of those adorning the hangars of other B-2As at Whiteman, features vertical red and white bars, a top view of the bomber and the blue sillouette of the characteristic shape of the State of Texas.

14
B-2A 88-0332 *SPIRIT OF WASHINGTON*, 325th BS/ 509th BW, Whiteman AFB, June 1995
The fourth operational B-2A to be delivered to the USAF, *SPIRIT OF WASHINGTON* received its name as an honour to the staff of the Boeing Company, who played a major, if sometimes unsung, role in the aircraft's development. Boeing was responsible for the B-2A's fuel systems, weapons delivery systems and landing gear, which, coincidentally was based upon that used for the 767 airliner. Some structural components, including the outboard and aft-centre sections of the fuselage, were also constructed within Boeing's massive manufacturing plants in Seattle.

15
B-2A 88-0330 *SPIRIT OF CALIFORNIA*, 13th BS/ 509th BW, Whiteman AFB, December 2005
The second B-2A to be delivered to Whiteman was Block 10 jet *SPIRIT OF CALIFORNIA*. Following the aircraft's arrival on 17 August 1994, 88-0330 performed a test flight on 23 September during which it conducted the first ever munition drop by a Spirit on the Utah Training and Test Range. The aircraft delivered two inert 2000-lb Mk 84 bombs on the range. On 11 December 1995, *SPIRIT OF CALIFORNIA* escorted *SPIRIT OF GEORGIA* back to Whiteman after its naming ceremony. 88-0330's flight on this date marked the 509th sortie performed by the 509th BW.

16
B-2A 89-0128 *SPIRIT OF NEBRASKA*, 393rd BS/ 509th BW, Whiteman AFB, September 1995
This planform view of 89-0128 *SPIRIT OF NEBRASKA* illustrates the complex flap arrangement on the aft side of the wings, as well as the hidden engine inlets. The aircraft is also painted in a blue-grey colour, and is not black as more commonly thought.

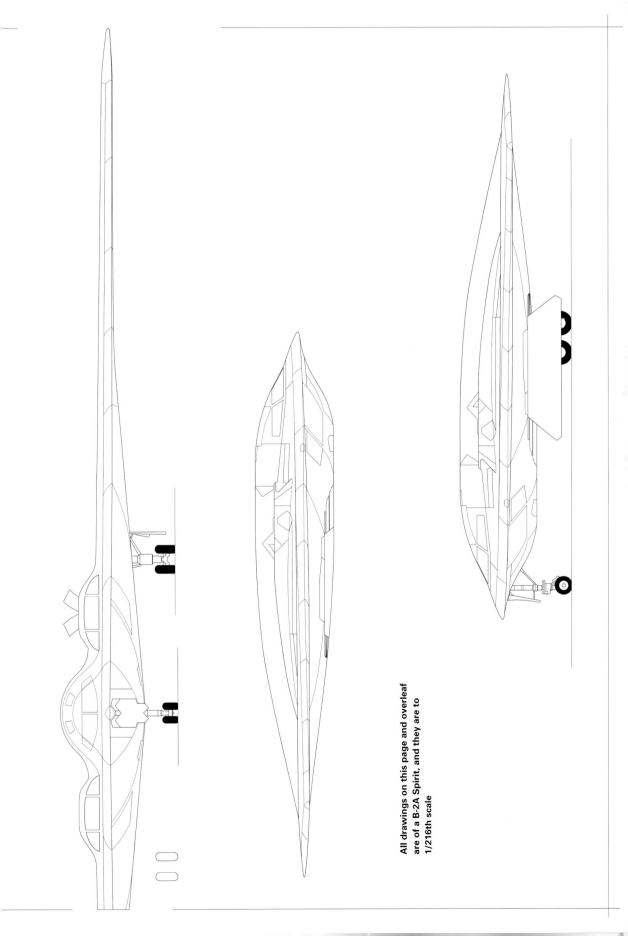

All drawings on this page and overleaf are of a B-2A Spirit, and they are to 1/216th scale

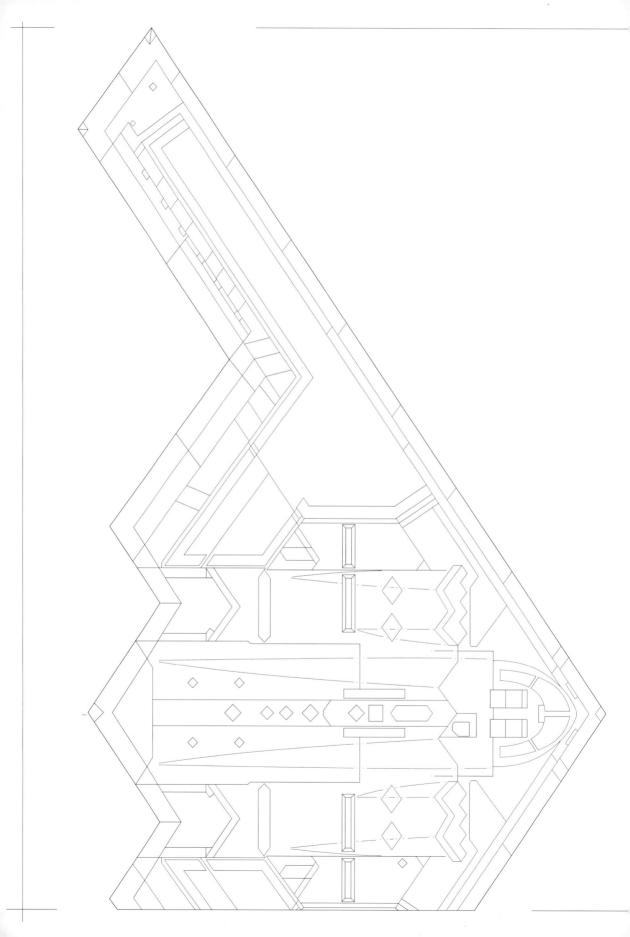

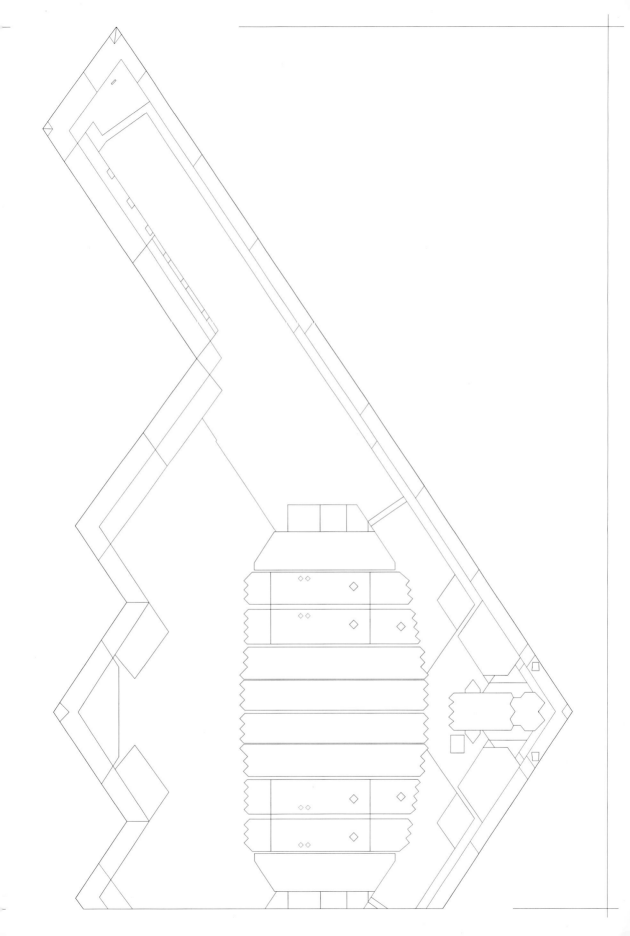

INDEX

References to illustrations are shown in **bold**. Plates are shown with page and caption locators in brackets.